- ENDORSEME?

In today's society, it is difficult for many authors to share their life experiences with the world and be translucent. Patricia Harris's chronicle and voyage of life, as written in her book *Imprisoned by Secrets of the Heart,* should be read as a source for those who are dealing with the pains of life's circumstances and calamities. The antidotes and solutions portrayed in this book serve as a guide for deliverance and healing of the mind, soul, and spirit.

PAUL JONES
T. D. JAKES MINISTRIES

Patricia Harris is a woman who has found freedom from the shame of her past. She is transparent in revealing her past mistakes so that others may experience the same forgiveness that she has received. As you read her book, you will laugh, cry, and rejoice, because in the end Satan is defeated once again. This book is also a call to those of us in leadership to take responsibility for our actions and walk in righteousness and purity....Thank you, Patricia, for sharing your story; because you have been forgiven much, it is evident that you love much!

JONI LAMB
DAYSTAR TELEVISION NETWORK

This is a book about change and restoration. Patricia shares her story with great honesty and transparency so that others may be set free from the past. May it bring the darkest places of your life into the light and love of Jesus Christ.

KATHY HAYES
SENIOR PASTOR, COVENANT CHURCH
DALLAS, TX

IMPRISONED
by Secrets
of the Heart

IMPRISONED
by Secrets
of the Heart

Patricia Harris

Whitaker House

IMPRISONED BY SECRETS OF THE HEART

Patricia Harris Ministries
P.O. Box 111103
Carrollton, TX 75011-1103
E-mail: imprisonedpch@aol.com
Website: www.handmaidensforhim.com

ISBN: 0-88368-624-4
Printed in the United States of America
Copyright © 2000 by Patricia C. Harris

Whitaker House
30 Hunt Valley Circle
New Kensington, PA 15068

Library of Congress Cataloging-in-Publication Data

Harris, Patricia C., 1958–
  Imprisoned by secrets of the heart / by Patricia C. Harris.
      p. cm.
Includes bibliographical references.
  ISBN 0-88368-624-4 (alk. paper)
  1. Harris, Patricia C., 1958– 2. Christian biography—United States.
I. Title.
  BR1725.H235 A3 2000
  277.3'0825'092—dc21
                                      00-009654

1 2 3 4 5 6 7 8 9 10 11 12 / 09 08 07 06 05 04 03 02 01 00

CONTENTS

Dedication 9

Foreword 11

Preface...15

Introduction 19

Section One: The Fall of (Wo)man.......................................23

1. Imprisoned Within..25

2. The Divorce...35

3. The Seed...39

4. The Affair...43

5. The Meeting 51

Section Two: God's Grace 59

6. The Quandary..61

7. The Prodigal Daughter 65

8. God's Princess...71

9. My Knight in Shining Armor 77

10. God's Amazing Grace...83

11. The Past Returns...89

12. The Unexpected..93

13. The Presence of Evil...97

14. The Letter..107

15. Secrets of the Heart 109

16. Tension in the Camp...115

17. My Alabaster Box 119

Section Three: Hope and a Future 123

18. Saturated with His Word 125

19. The Audible Voice of God..131

20. The Powerless Veil of Shame..135

21. Unashamed 137

Section Four: Free at Last...143

22. Hurting People, Healed Lives 145

23. Happily Ever After...157

24. KEYS to Your Freedom...161

Prayers of Agreement for Healing and Restoration.....................175

    A Prayer Reflecting God's Faithfulness 176

    A Prayer for the Imprisoned Heart.............................177

    A Prayer of Repentance for the Single 179

    A Prayer for Self-Forgiveness..................................180

    A Prayer of Displacement 182

    A Prayer for Destroying Soul-Ties.............................183

Afterword to the Reader 185

Acknowledgments 187

About the Author 191

Dedication

Foremost, I dedicate this book to my precious heavenly Father; my Lord and Savior, Jesus Christ; and the Holy Spirit who comforted me while I was "imprisoned."

Second, I wish to dedicate this book to my godly husband and the priest of our home, Eddie Harris, whose unconditional love served as the impetus I needed to begin my journey to wholeness. I love you with all my heart.

To my parents, Bill and Mary Cunningham: Thank you for always being there. Both of you stood beside me as I began my pilgrimage to wholeness. I want to thank you for believing in me enough to make an investment in the telling of my story. The original version of the book was a result of the seed you sowed. I love you both so much.

To my three children, Denyel, Earl, and Amira, I say thank you for allowing me to write this book. Your father and I are especially grateful for your unified prayers that this written work will serve as an anointed conduit to heal hurting lives. I love you and thank you for your support.

Finally, I dedicate this book to each woman whose life parallels my own painful indiscretions and moral failings. I pray that you may experience wholeness, that you may be transformed into the likeness of Father God, who created you with purpose and dignity. In the presence of God, and by the authority of Jesus Christ, I declare that you shall be set free! The chains are broken! You, too, are free to be "the unashamed woman" through the atoning blood of Jesus!

Dance before His presence with great joy, bow at His feet and adore Him, for He adores you and He loves you with an *"everlasting love"* (Jeremiah 31:3). You are His princess, His jewel, and the sparkle in His eye.

Foreword

DR. WANDA DAVIS-TURNER
President, Calling First Ladies, Inc.
Author, Speaker, Recording Artist

It's not often that one has an opportunity to pick up a book and, in a matter of hours, walk through twelve years of another's pain, sorrow, shame, grief, and anger, and yet, before one even gets near the last page, to sense the marvelous redemptive work of Christ in this precious vessel's life.

Patricia Harris has uniquely captured the heart of Jesus as He is invited into the most horrible, sorrowful, and painful times of life—when we disappoint God, family, friends, and ourselves. Instead of rejection, Patricia's story reflects God's love and forgiveness. Instead of anger, Patricia's story reflects God's pity and love. Instead of sorrow, Patricia's story reflects God's joy when we allow Him to turn the most horrible circumstances of life into the most redemptive, miraculous, and victorious celebration.

I was so blessed as I was quickly given the opportunity not only to share Patricia's testimony, but to identify those moments that all of us experience when it becomes so hard to forgive ourselves and to believe that, no matter what we have committed, God has already made provisions to forgive and restore us. *Imprisoned by Secrets of the Heart* is kin to all of us. "Imprisoned" is where we've all traveled. Becoming the bride of Christ is where we're all headed! Thanks, Patricia, for showing us the way.

JESSYE RUFFIN
Associate Pastor
Covenant Church, Dallas, TX

The Lord's desire is for every person to possess his own soul with His steadfastness of heart. (See Luke 21:19.) I have known Patricia Harris for ten years as her spiritual counselor. I have stood by her as she recovered her soul from the contamination of the Enemy. I have observed her forge through all of Satan's schemes against her and be victorious. There were times when she felt as if she couldn't take any more attacks, but as she has now learned, it took all of her trials and tribulations to build the honorable character and deep fortitude of soul that she possesses. If she were to take away even a microscopic portion of her life, she would not be the tremendous spiritual warrior for the Gospel that she is. It took all of her past emotional pain and heartache in order for the Holy Spirit to fashion her into the shining light that she has become.

Many of us have a shameful past that we are not proud of, but few of us have the courage and strength to sacrificially help others by writing about it in a book. Patricia is a very courageous woman of God who felt that if Jesus could die on the cross for mankind's reconciliation to the Father, then she could bear the cross of writing this book about not only her failures with the Enemy, but also her great victories over the Enemy.

Satan's desire was to strip Patricia of all her self-esteem and God-esteem in the area of how she perceived herself as a woman of God. The Enemy attacks women and men daily, and he lies to them about what they think about themselves, what others think of them, and how the Lord perceives them. If the Enemy can strip us of our identity in God, then he can strip us of the God within us and pervert our purpose for being. And if he needs to use a man of God to carry out his schemes against us, he will.

Satan was unsuccessful in his war against Patricia and Eddie, and he will be unsuccessful in his attack against you. Patricia's story will provoke you to repent and turn away from the supposed safety of sensual living on those dead-end streets of life or the safety you are seeking in whatever hidden hurt or shame you're embracing. These avenues in life have been diabolically created by Satan, whose only goal is to destroy you.

I believe that, through this book, many people will be set free from their own private hurts and shame. Women and men will be set free from attacks against their identity in God. These attacks are targeted at the essence of how we reflect God, since we were created in His image.

We need all that Jesus has for us. Jesus came to set all of us free from the bondage of sin, and He is the only way to recovery.

Preface

As I first began to write this book, I struggled with the fact that its contents would expose in startling detail the shameful acts I performed against God, against the body of Christ, and against my family, all of whom I love very much.

Inwardly, I remained unresolved regarding my decision to disclose my wretched, twelve-year secret. During this time of indecision, my thoughts drifted back to how, in the midst of my turmoil, I had often yearned to read a book written by a godly woman who had traveled the same agonizing path that I had experienced firsthand. I longed to scan the shelves of a Christian bookstore and find available resources and reading material by another woman like myself—a woman who actually overcame the shame, disgrace, and condemnation of sexual impurity.

Dear reader, the impurity to which I refer was an impurity that I willfully chose after I became a Christian. No, nobody snatched my purity from me, nor can I honestly attribute prior family background or even ignorance as justification for my subsequent descent into the debauchery and forbidden lust of the flesh that I permitted into my life. Rather, as a woman of God, born again and spirit filled, I chose to forsake my purity and my relationship with God for an adulterous relationship with a married man—a married man who was, in fact, my pastor.

I have repeatedly struggled with the disclosure of my painful past while writing these solemn words. Yet I have also simultaneously sensed victory in my spirit—victory that I now boldly proclaim rises upon the horizon for countless women seeking shelter from the same storms that assailed my own life, and for others who are struggling to overcome equally painful types of shame and hurt that they've experienced in their lives.

For those of you who read the words of this book and who can relate personally or indirectly to my story, yes, undoubtedly, we did defile ourselves. We have, in fact, experienced moral and spiritual failure in our lives; as a result, we have hurt our loved ones, ourselves, and our heavenly Father. And, yes, many of us have lived with insufferable guilt, deep-seated pain, and self-condemnation because of it. But I declare to you this moment, in spite of all this, because of Christ's shed blood on Calvary, you can be adorned in a veil of glory if you are willing to release all of your past to Him.

There are many types of "imprisonment." You may not have experienced the same moral or spiritual failure that I did, but you may be in bondage to something else — drugs, alcohol, pornography, the pain of divorce, abuse, even self-pity or rejection — and it is keeping you from living the life of freedom God has provided for you. You also can be set free in victory, because the same truths of redemption, forgiveness, and restoration apply to us all. The principles in this book will bring you renewed hope and help to set you free.

That is why, regardless of the option available to me to maintain anonymity and forego the writing of the following pages, I have chosen instead to boldly pen the subsequent chapters in obedience to God's voice. He has inspired me to write my story as a testimony so that others might overcome their own guilt, shame, and condemnation. In actuality, *Imprisoned by Secrets of the Heart* is from Him to every hurting woman who has ever experienced the shame of sexual impurity at any level, and to all who struggle with their own types of imprisonment.

While reviewing this book again, I became emotional because of the great work God has done in my life, but also because of what I feel He will do in others' lives to set them free. This book, in essence, is the book I searched the bookshelves for but never found. The book was in *me* all along. The book I longed to read, of a woman's exit out of her shame, was within me all that time. And now it is about to be made available to many other "imprisoned" people who have probably been searching the shelves for the very same book. I am overwhelmed that He chose me to be the vessel through which it came.

Preface

To those who are or have been entangled in a stronghold of lust or infidelity, or who may even be on the verge of making such a decision; to all who feel entrapped by their own personal sins and failures, God has ordained that this book be written for you. No longer do you have to bear the weight of your shame.

You can truly be free through Jesus!

—PATRICIA HARRIS

Introduction

This book represents the true, startling, revelatory account of how I, a Christian, wounded, betrayed, scarred with genital herpes, and a single parent of two little children aged three and four, walked away from a ten-year physically and emotionally abusive marriage—only to become involved in sexual sin. Poor decisions, immense vulnerability, and my innate willingness to believe the Devil's lies sent me headlong into a sexual relationship with my pastor—scarring me in such a way that it would hinder God's anointing in my life. Consequently, I would carry the weight of that guilt for twelve long years. Feeling inadequate, dirty, and worthless, I invisibly wallowed under the overwhelming, ominous clouds of heaviness, self-reproach, guilt, shame, and condemnation. When I ultimately found the strength to sever the relationship with my pastor, I had nowhere to go, no one to turn to. My immediate family (parents and siblings), always so supportive, were a thousand miles away in other states. I felt so alone.

I believe that the denigrating shame associated with sexual impurity is one that women find hard to face because it demeans the "lady" in them. Ladies are viewed as pure, graceful, gentle, kind, wholesome, sound, polite, gracious, adorable, neat, well adorned,...and the list goes on. So how can a woman who has committed an act of sexual impurity, especially with a married man, ever feel that she deserves the right to be called a "lady"? Even worse, how can she overcome her feelings of self-condemnation when that act occurred with a married man who was also her pastor?

Somehow, I told myself that I could get over it—that it was behind me now, that it wasn't all my fault. Yet for years I carried the burden and the shame inside a broken vessel. Nevertheless, God kept on loving me and never gave up on my future.

Because I didn't know who I was in Christ, I felt as though I were just a number, a person without a name—a prisoner. One of Satan's greatest plans is to deceive us by clouding our view of who God says we are in His Word. Being greatly deceived, I bought the Devil's lies that I was an insignificant being, that I didn't have value.

However, I later learned something that put a new perspective on my feeling that I was just a number. I discovered that certain numbers could be powerful statements, from God's perspective. The Bible uses numbers that are symbolic in the heart of God. For example, the numbers two, five, and nine are relevant to my twelve-year journey. According to the book *Number in Scripture*,[1] the number two refers to the fall of man, five is the number of grace or favor for the unworthy, and nine symbolizes the conclusion of a matter. In essence, this numerical combination summarizes the events that took place in my life—a *fallen* woman experienced the *grace* of God and the *victorious conclusion* to a twelve-year, private imprisonment. Thus, the numbers two, five, and nine can be significant to all of us. Although you may have fallen, there is yet God's bountiful grace by which your conclusion can be victorious through Christ Jesus.

So when Satan tries to tell you that you are just a number, tell him that you know where you've been and you know where you're going, and, unlike his case, your conclusion will end in victory through the redemptive blood of Jesus!

Today, I am a victorious overcomer, and God wants the same for you! I would like to share with you the journey I traveled from my veil of shame to my veil of glory. As you read my story, you will see how the hand of God guided me. God cares just as much for your victory as He does for mine, no matter what your particular situation, mistakes, or failures. My triumphs can be your triumphs, too. I ask that you envision yourself coming out of your situation with a shout of victory. As the song by Rich Mullins says, "God is an awesome God. He reigns from heaven above with wisdom, power, and love." He is such an awesome God. He cares for you and me.

---

[1] See E. W. Bullinger, *Number in Scripture* (Grand Rapids, MI: Kregel Publications, 1967).

For I know the thoughts and plans that I have for you, says the
Lord, thoughts and plans for welfare and peace and not for evil, to
give you hope in your final outcome.
—Jeremiah 29:11 AMP

For your [former] shame you shall have a twofold recompense;
instead of dishonor and reproach [your people] shall rejoice in
their portion. Therefore in their land they shall possess double
[what they had forfeited]; everlasting joy shall be theirs.
—Isaiah 61:7 AMP

There is therefore now no condemnation to those who are in
Christ Jesus, who do not walk according to the flesh, but
according to the Spirit.
—Romans 8:1

Section One:
The Fall of (Wo)man

Chapter One

Imprisoned Within

Y ou probably think you're alone in your anguish, but you're not. You have a dark secret—one you buried in the deepest recesses of your heart, one you vowed you would never reveal to another living soul, one that makes you cringe every time you think about it. Or you have a deep-seated hurt or pain through no fault of your own, and the memory of it lingers and is paralyzing your life.

You have tried to forget it, but you can't. You've done everything you can think of to get rid of it, but you haven't. Whether it's from hurt, shame, guilt, condemnation, or fear, we all struggle with inner imprisonment at some time or other. I know. I've been there.

You can't always tell a person's imprisonment by outward appearance or behavior. A person can wear a smile and still be imprisoned. You can be the person labeled "most likely to succeed" but be held captive to your past. On the other hand, you can withdraw and avoid people—even life itself—and try to hide your private shame. But the result is the same—pain and isolation. It is the imprisonment of the heart. It is the hidden place.

But there is very good news for those of us who have been trapped in the prisons of our private pain and shame: God has a heart for the imprisoned. As a matter of fact, Jesus specifically addressed people who are imprisoned. He stated,

The Spirit of the Lord [is] upon Me, because He has anointed Me [the Anointed One, the Messiah] to preach the good news (the Gospel) to the poor; He has sent Me to announce release to the

captives [the "imprisoned" population, author's insertion],...*those...[who are downtrodden, bruised, crushed, and broken down by calamity], to proclaim the accepted and acceptable year of the Lord [the day when salvation and the free favors of God profusely abound].*   (Luke 4:18–19 AMP)

And in Isaiah, the message is further proclaimed:

To grant [consolation and joy] to those who mourn in Zion – to give them an ornament...of beauty instead of ashes, the oil of joy instead of mourning, the garment [expressive] of praise instead of a heavy, burdened, and failing spirit – that they may be called oaks of righteousness [lofty, strong, and magnificent, distinguished for uprightness, justice, and right standing with God], the planting of the Lord, that He may be glorified....Instead of your [former] shame you shall have a twofold recompense; instead of dishonor and reproach [your people] shall rejoice in their portion. Therefore in their land they shall possess double [what they had forfeited]; everlasting joy shall be theirs.   (Isaiah 61:3, 7 AMP)

Isn't that exciting? The above Scriptures share with us the plans God has for those who are "imprisoned," and what their future holds. God has already developed a great restoration plan for the ex-prisoner, for the person who is no longer bound by his or her agonizing prison walls. Once you experience the bountiful, unconditional love that can only be imparted by God's grace and understood by the Spirit, you will then transition into walking in the profusely abounding free favors of God! You will be given consolation and joy, beauty instead of ashes, joy instead of mourning, praise instead of a failing spirit, and will be called oaks of righteousness – distinguished for uprightness! And, instead of shame, there will be double honor, and all that was lost will be given in a double measure.

I am a witness of the truths that are spoken in these passages of Scripture. Compared to the twelve years that I lost in captivity, I have been doubly blessed with honor. My ashes have been turned to beauty, my mourning to joy! I can dance again!

Perhaps you are being held captive against your will. You desire to be free from the prison walls that surround you, yet your inner self says that such freedom could never be yours, that it could never happen for you because of the depth of your sorrow, your sin, or your failure. Daily, you are tormented with the pain that nags at your soul. You wear the face of ease, but inwardly, your shame, guilt, and condemnation seem more than you can bear. As a matter of fact, they are unbearable! And you are tired of carrying them everywhere you go. "Why have they stayed with me so long?" you ask. "All these months, years, all this time. Will the memory of it all ever subside?"

Are these the questions that keep replaying in your mind? Be assured that God knows your pain, your suffering, and your sorrow. He has a redemptive plan in place for you—one that will free you totally and forever! I can hear you say, "But how? How can I receive and benefit from this redemptive plan? I have struggled with being 'imprisoned' for years. I want to be free, but I still find myself being held captive!"

Those are the same nagging questions and the same emotional tailspins that stabbed at my heart every time I would make an attempt to "lay it on the altar" and give it to God. My problem was this: I did not feel it was Jesus' responsibility to handle the mess I had created. I knew He had forgiven me for my failures, and I appreciated it, but yet I felt it was still my cross to bear. Perhaps if I had been an unbeliever at the time of my sordid sin, I could have accepted the redemptive plan without question. After all, when unbelievers make mistakes, it is understandable, because that's what sinners do. But that was not my issue. I was, in fact, a born-again believer. I had already experienced the love of Jesus, and I knew of His sufferings for my sins. As a "fallen woman" with a past that yet lurked behind every memory, I simply had made up my mind that I would not allow Jesus to suffer again for me. I felt that I had had my chance to walk uprightly, and that, to put it simply, I had flat-out blown it. Therefore, I would do the suffering. I had to pay the price for my failure, not Jesus.

Every time the pain of my past would lift up its ugly head, I decided I would shed the tears, not Jesus. When the load seemed immensely heavy and overbearing, I would rearrange my baggage so I could somehow manage the weight and continue to carry it. I refused to let Jesus be my Burden-Bearer. Over and over again, I internalized this way of thinking: "It's my fault, my past, my failures, my pain, my shame, my guilt, and my condemnation—I will just have to live with it!" God's enemy, Satan, fed these lies to me daily, and I accepted them as truth.

However, when we think like this, we are saying that God's redemptive plan through His Son Jesus is just not good enough for us. We are deciding to make ourselves bigger than Jesus by getting on the cross to hang and to pay for the punishment of our own sins. But you and I both know that there is only One who was fit to be slaughtered as the Sacrifice and who could pay for the sins of the world. No matter how noble we may think we are by trying to be our own burden-carrier, we cannot begin to handle the weight of our past failures or pain. God did not create man to bear his own sins, much less anyone else's.

I concluded one day that I was either going to believe the Word of God as truth, or I was going to doubt its power as it pertained to me. Either I was redeemed by the blood, or I was going to reject its claims. Either the mercy seat was for me, or I was going to deny its purpose. Either I was going to totally trust God, or I was going to trust myself.

It seemed so scary at first as I began to review my options—believing the Word, being redeemed by the power in the blood, accepting the purpose of the mercy seat, and trusting God. As I reviewed each option, they all pointed to the same truth. I was going to have to bear my soul to God. All that I was and ever hoped to be would have to lie open before Him so that I could allow Him to come close to me and see into the deepest parts of my being.

My first response was, "No! You can't go there!"—because in the deepest parts of my being was a place called Shame, and its neighborhood was made up of ugly memories. "I don't want You to see them; this place is disarrayed, it's ugly, it's not for Your eyes to see!" I rationalized with God.

David said,

> If I ascend up into heaven, You are there; if I make my bed in Sheol (the place of the dead), behold, You are there. If I take the

wings of the morning or dwell in the uttermost parts of the sea, even there shall Your hand lead me, and Your right hand shall hold me....Even the darkness hides nothing from You, but the night shines as the day; the darkness and the light are both alike to You....Where could I go from Your Spirit? Or where could I flee from Your presence? (Psalm 139:8–10, 12, 7 AMP)

I had to realize that God knew my sorrow and that, in the midst of my pain, in the midst of my past sins, He had always been there, and that nothing was hidden from Him.

How could I hide anything from God? David said He is everywhere, and even the darkness is light to Him. So here I was, faced with the decision to be intimate with God. To be intimate with Him meant I had to let down my guard. I would have to trust Him with my whole life (body, spirit, and soul)—which, up to this point, had been self-governed. I was faced with the challenge of letting Him bring light to the darkest area of my soul, the area that I had never let Him touch because I was too ashamed to let Him go there. It was this dark area of my life that had kept me from knowing Him in His fullness.

In the Bible, when a man would "know" a woman, it meant that he became intimate with her. I had prevented intimacy from happening between God and myself because I did not want Him to know me. In reality, He already did. However, like a gentleman, He was waiting for me to give Him the invitation to come in and know me. God is not pushy, nor will He push His Son Jesus into our lives. But when we are ready, He stands at the door knocking, and all He has to hear is, "Come in."

I made what I thought was the most difficult decision I could ever make in my life. I decided to pull back the covers from the darkest place of my heart. I made up my mind to trust Him. I asked God to give me the grace to forgive myself, because I knew that I was holding myself captive as I allowed Satan to make me believe I was unworthy. I was at a point in my life where I knew I was ready to let go. Have you come to that point in your life? Are you there? How long have you been on your journey? Has it been weeks, months, years, a lifetime? Any length of time is too long.

There is a redemptive plan that has been put in place to set the captives free. It's time to trust the Word of God. Jesus said, "I came that you might have life, and that more abundantly." (See John 10:10.) Is your life abundant today, or are you still a prisoner? Jesus wants to be your Burden-Bearer. His shed blood can make it possible for you to have a clean slate; your sins will be no more.

I made the decision to stand exposed before Him. All that I was, the pitiful me, with all my hidden secrets, wanted to be free. I remembered women from the Bible: the woman with the alabaster box, the woman caught in adultery, and the woman at the well. Jesus loved each of them. In their most vulnerable states, they opened up to Him as His eyes met theirs and as His heart identified with their pain. These women bared their souls, and He changed their lives.

Since I had already lost twelve years of my life, I felt it was worth the risk. I invited Him in. I did the very thing I thought I would never, ever do, because I felt so much shame. I let Jesus come into the hidden region of my soul where He could see it all—nothing hidden.

As I let Him in, vivid pictures of the pastor with whom I'd had the affair raced through my mind, and then suddenly I experienced the finality of the shame, the guilt, the condemnation, the sorrow, and the agonizing tears of my past. Amazingly, the darkest area of my life had light! For the first time in twelve years, I knew I was a *free* woman! An amazing transformation had taken place in my life. There are no words descriptive enough to accurately explain what suddenly happened to me—in a matter of seconds. Just moments before, I had struggled with a past that had haunted me into believing that captivity was my destiny; but now here I sat, with tearstained eyes, gloriously changed by the hand of a willing Father who had been waiting for me to give Him the invitation to know me.

Will you allow Jesus to know you, too? You can be a born-again believer and yet not be intimate with the Father. Pastor Kathy Hayes (my pastor's wife at Covenant Church in Dallas, Texas, where I now attend) so perfectly explained the word *intimacy* when she said, "Intimacy simply means 'Into me see.'"

When a husband and wife are intimate without reservation, they are saying to one another, "I lay down my sword, and I give you my coat in exchange for your coat. That means that I am vulnerable before you. I have nothing to hide and no weapon to protect myself with." The exchange of coats represents the covenant vows of their marriage. The husband and wife are saying to each other, "Into me see" — and then there is the "knowing." Will you say to our Father God, "Into me see"? Will you take the challenge of trusting Him and standing naked before Him? He waits to be invited; He is a gentleman and will not push His way to the forefront of your life. But, should you truly know Him, you will reap the joy of His abundant grace and mercy as He reigns supreme in you and through you.

Because I opened my heart to God, my life will never be the same. Today, I walk in liberty as I help others to achieve their freedom. Be blessed and allow God to be God, and He will do amazing "suddenlys" in your life, too.

You can walk in freedom no matter what type of imprisonment you are struggling with. Once, at a book signing, I met a young married man, the father of two, who came up to my table with a sincere look of longing. His comments to me were that he desired to be free from the stronghold of drugs in his life. He stated that he loved the Lord, yet he had struggled with this addiction for years. He desperately reached for my book in hopes of finding an avenue to his freedom. His wife later approached my table as her husband continued to pour out his heart. I imparted words of hope and life to both of them.

I recognized that this man had a generational problem that needed to be broken in his life before he could be set free. God can do a supernatural work in our lives and cause us to walk in a glorious transformation. But even so, we still need to address, by the Spirit, strongholds in our family backgrounds. I was able to explain to this man's local church leaders the processes necessary for obtaining deliverance from these strongholds, and I provided them with resource information for training in spiritual warfare, so that they could help many others, as well. We must know how to war against the Enemy; it is imperative!

Another person whom I remember so well was a young girl who had chosen a life of promiscuity. Having been mistreated by both parents when she was a child, she had lost her identity and had chosen the lifestyle of a lesbian. However, she was seeking to be free to know who she was and why she was created. She and I were able to talk on at least two occasions, and she continued to struggle with letting go of her past and allowing God to lead her into her future. This woman sincerely loved God and wanted her purpose in God to be fulfilled. I could see by the Spirit that the Enemy had thwarted her life and caused it to take a divergent course. However, I believe this woman will be redirected into the plan of God. I sometimes weep because I want everyone to be as free as I am and to experience it now. But I know my limitations; it is not within me to make things happen. It is within me to share and impart God's truth and then to allow God to move by His Spirit. Therefore, I submit everyone to the heart of the Father.

A very dear student of mine, who attended the class that I teach called "Shame to Glory," struggled with the memory of an abusive spouse who severely abused her and her children. By the grace of God, she escaped from the abusive home, but not without physical and emotional scarring. For years, she wanted him to pay for all the pain he had caused her and her children. But also by the grace of God, this woman was able to stand open and exposed before Him and allow Him to know her. Today, this woman moves about with more liberty than I have ever seen in her before.

In one of my classes, I had several ladies who struggled with the pain of not having had a loving mother to care for them and nurture them as they grew older. Their mothers had abandoned their roles as "mom," and each woman was dealing with her own individual pain of not only having missed the "mother factor," but also the "father factor." As these women courageously shared their stories with one another in the class, they each realized there were others who shared similar pain. God began to use each to minister healing to the others. Bonds were formed, and God began His transforming work as these women opened the darkest part of their souls.

I have ministered to women who have been molested by male relatives, women who struggle with the issue of their husbands' leaving them for another woman, women who have been the mistress of a pastor, pastors' wives who have experienced the pain of their husbands' affairs, women who carry the guilt of abortion, women who are presently engaged in or have been engaged in illicit affairs, women who have had a child by a married man, women who have been raped, women and men of all backgrounds who struggle with being "imprisoned."

One of the most precious stories that still brings tears to my eyes is that of a pastor's wife who visited with me after a ladies' conference where I was the guest speaker. I will never forget her name or her precious spirit. This pastor's wife came up to me and began to share that she, too, had experienced the pain of having a husband who had an affair with a young woman in the church. She said that her husband became very ill shortly thereafter and that she now cares for him at home. She said that when the sin was discovered, this young girl fled the church. The pastor's wife said she heard that this young lady was struggling with the shame of her affair and could not bear to face the church or the pastor's wife. This precious woman began to weep as she looked into my eyes. She said that she desired to find this sister and to hug her. She said that if she could hug her and tell her how much she loved her and forgave her, she believed this would bring healing to the young lady's life. She shook her head and said, "Sometimes I wonder where she is and if she is okay. I just wish I could hug her."

In that moment, as she said those words, I began to weep as well, and I asked her if it would be all right if I stood in the gap for that young lady. I told her she could hug me. This pastor's wife reached out her arms and embraced me as I laid my head on her shoulder and wept. Together, we held each other, and God ministered to us both as I stood in the gap for the woman who had betrayed her, and (little did she know) as she stood in the gap for the pastor's wife whom I had betrayed. Then this lady kissed me and blessed me, and prophetically told me, "Someday I am going to see you on television. You are going to set a lot of women free." It remains obvious to me that this woman walks in freedom. She has dealt with her pain, her disappointment, and the issue of forgiveness. I will never forget this woman; she touched a place in my heart forever.

God has a plan to use your past for His glory. Satan has a plan to destroy your life with your past. God's love draws you to

Him. Satan tries to pull you away from God. The Bible says that we do not wrestle against flesh and blood but against principalities in high places. To do this, we must put on the whole armor of God. (See Ephesians 6:12–18.)

As a trained leader in the healing and deliverance ministry at my church, I value every opportunity God gives me to help people exit from their pasts. It is my reasonable service unto Him (Romans 12:1). God's plan is for all of us to walk in freedom so we can destroy the works of darkness and put Satan's kingdom under our feet!

In the following pages, you'll read of both my imprisonment and my journey to freedom. Because I was trapped in the prison of pain and shame, I know what you're now going through. And because I've experienced freedom, I know that you, too, can experience a joy-filled new life as you break free from the secrets of your heart.

Chapter Two

The Divorce

L ike many young girls, I dreamed of growing up, getting married to a tall, dark, and handsome "knight in shining armor," raising children, and living happily ever after. During my adolescence, my thoughts often drifted to such a make-believe, fantasy world. In my spare moments, I would write countless short stories in which my main characters—usually a young, beautiful girl and a knight in shining armor—would marry at the plot's conclusion and live long, fulfilling, prosperous lives.

I believed that I had finally fulfilled my dreams when I married my high school sweetheart at the tender age of nineteen. My marriage, however, failed to be the fantasy I envisioned as a child. I found myself married to a very wounded man, a man who was hurting from unmet needs in his childhood. There were so many unresolved issues: the premature death of his mother while he was yet a little boy; a grieving, alcoholic father who had abdicated his parental responsibilities; and, additionally, the loss of what had once been a close-knit family but that was tragically divided throughout his childhood and adolescent years.

After nine years of an abusive marital relationship to this man, I became a divorcée with two small children, with financial indebtedness and immense, insufferable, emotional baggage. With only a year of college and limited skills, I joined one of the fastest growing groups in the country—single parents.

Prior to our divorce, my husband, whom I will call Fred Weaver, and I had sought marital counseling from our pastor. This same pastor, incidentally, had also provided pastoral leadership to my husband and me when we lived in another state. Amid several years of job relocations and transfers, our paths crossed, and, once again, we found ourselves attending his church. As a result of those years of mutual acquaintance, we had fostered a friendship with this pastor and his wife.

Though Fred and I had previously pursued secular counseling, no tangible results or noticeable change had occurred in our marriage. No matter which counselor I selected, Fred expressed open disdain, disinterest, and an unwillingness to be transparent. In fact, he even indicated his disinterest in seeking marital guidance from our pastor. However, in this instance, I unflinchingly insisted that both he and I pursue pastoral counseling if we were to save our dangling-by-a-thread marriage.

So, with Fred reluctantly in tow, we attended several counseling sessions with the pastor and his wife. Even when his wife was unable to attend, the pastor would still meet with the two of us. It appeared, however, to be a losing battle. Eventually, I reported Fred to the authorities for his continued physical violence. He was later removed from our home, and I found myself alone with our two small children.

My family, made aware of the marital separation, tried to offer as much support as possible. My mother, a devoted believer and a praying woman, would call, pray for me, and counsel me long distance. My parents, as well as my siblings, sent money to assist me in my financial struggles. They helped as much as they could, but they all lived far away. Now, alone and a thousand miles from home, I faced feelings of rejection and abandonment, and the debilitating aftermath of an emotionally draining and physically abusive marriage.

Additionally, the infidelity introduced into our marriage by Fred, and then my subsequent infidelity, had left me with a severe case of genital herpes. Before our marriage dissolved, I discovered that Fred was a carrier and that I had contracted the dreadful disease from him. In all honesty, I could not place all of the blame on him, as we were both guilty of extramarital affairs and, as a result, were reaping what we had sown. So, here I was, not only a single parent of a four-year-old daughter and three-year-old son, but also a battered casualty of an abusive marriage, left wounded, betrayed, and scarred with genital herpes. Unfortunately, from this point on, I would continue to make poor decisions, the consequences of which I would bear for years to come.

The Divorce

Where do I go? Is there anywhere to hide?
I feel lonely, afraid, so barren inside.
With my two little ones I desperately roam
Looking for a place I can call my true home.

Alone, yet not alone; God will lead the way;
Only He can guide my decisions each day.
But I decide to handle this all on my own.
I turn from God, and no longer seek His throne.

But pushing God away only makes things worse;
The spirit of darkness comes just like a curse.
Twelve years of imprisonment, shame, and disguise,
Pass slowly before I can finally arise...
to walk in Victory.

Chapter Three

The Seed

After my husband's removal from our home, the pastor who had provided ongoing counseling to us during our marital difficulties stopped by to check on my kids and me. Though not yet divorced, Fred had filed the papers to initiate the process, and I was in total agreement with his decision. I no longer desired to keep our destructive relationship together. It had become an effort in futility.

On one occasion, when the pastor, whom I will simply refer to as "Pastor," called me on the phone, he mentioned to me that his wife had accused him of being interested in me because of his continued involvement in my life. At that point, I had never even considered the thought. When I addressed him as "Pastor," I thought of him only in that regard. I was soon to discover, however, that Pastor had, in fact, thought of me beyond what was appropriate. When he stated to me what his wife was thinking, I felt a sense of embarrassment and told him, "Oh, no, that would be horrible." I suggested to the pastor that I talk with his wife to reassure her. At that time, my youth, naiveté, and immaturity clouded my perception, and I was unaware of the pastor's intentions toward me.

Though Pastor's wife was a radiant woman, I later found out that she was also very wounded and broken, and with good reason. She distrusted her husband and intentionally distanced herself from many women, including me. Though I had known her for years and was fond of her, she did not pursue a close relationship with me. Later, I would discover why.

Pastor, on the other hand, was quite the opposite. He was everyone's friend. He knew everyone, and everyone knew him. He was well liked by both men and women, and had garnered respect in the community. Overall, Pastor seemed to possess an enviable reputation. (I have since discovered the difference between reputation and character: reputation is who people think you are, while character is who you are when no one is looking.)

In addition to his being a pastor, he had previously held such prestigious positions as bishop, in which he had oversight over numerous churches. He also served as a board member of several reputable community organizations. Coupled with these outward accolades, Pastor possessed dynamic wit, charm, and charisma. He could mingle with any group and present his ideas and opinions with authority. As a result, he often successfully manipulated or exerted control in many situations. In the midst of her husband's unabashed popularity and favor, Pastor's wife would often stand by silently on the sidelines. She had evolved into a very insecure woman because, as I later discovered, Pastor's underlying ultimatum to her regarding his lifestyle was, "Either take it or leave it." Obviously, she had decided to "take it."

After Pastor had disclosed his wife's feelings and I had responded with denial that such a thing could occur, he inquired as to why I would think such a situation would be repugnant. He queried me with such questions as: "Do you think I am too old?" "Would it be that bad?" "What's wrong with me?" "Am I ugly?" And, with a chuckle, he would unabashedly add, "I know I am good lookin'." I flushed, embarrassed by his direct questioning.

Despite his candid questioning and comments, which caught me off guard, I was flattered that this man—not just a mere man, but the pastor—would consider me. (In retrospect, I now realize that this was due to my own intense inferiority complex, coupled with my unresolved, deep-seated, emotional baggage and my failure to realize who I was in Christ.) The seed of lust was planted in his heart, and the seed of turning to an illicit source for affirmation took form in mine. This would eventually lead to my spiraling descent into the throes of a forbidden affair and twelve years of self-condemnation.

Somebody Wants Me

What can these newfound feelings be
That have awakened within me?
Hope, intrigue, tender sympathy;
Feelings that somebody wants me,
Somebody really wants me.

Life seems sweeter than before.
It makes me embrace it all the more.
Powerful him and little me.
He's willing to risk it all—for me?
Somebody really wants me.

What makes him stop to look at me?
Who am I now that I should be
Given this chance to live again?
He really wants me, of all men,
Somebody really wants me.

He sweetly knocks upon my door,
How do I know what is in store?
My dead emotions come alive;
I think that now I can survive.
Somebody really wants me.

It feels good, but it doesn't.
  It seems right, but it isn't.
    I feel bold, yet ashamed.
      I want in, but I want out.
        I want to pray, but I can't.
          I know what I want,
            But am confused.
          I want to win,
              but am afraid I'll lose
                ...and, inwardly, I know it.

God is there, and so is Satan.
God is reaching,
Satan pulling.
God says, "Come";
Satan, "Don't listen."
God says, "Come";
Satan, "He's waiting."
God says, "Come";
Satan, "He wants you."

And I say…

What could these newfound feelings be?
That have awakened within me?
Soon in despair I'll quickly sink
Yet this is all that I can think:
Somebody really wants me.

Chapter Four

The Affair

After a few more visits from Pastor, the affair began. He knew that I had genital herpes because I had disclosed this very intimate detail to him during the prior marital counseling sessions. But he told me that he did not care. I was puzzled at his response concerning this incurable disease and the potential risk of transference.

The physical side of our illicit relationship began at his request and continued at his request. At first, I was really interested in the pastor as well. I was *"drawn away by* [my] *own desires and enticed"* (James 1:14). I looked forward to seeing him and being with him. However, eventually, the initial thrill went away, and the reality of my actions became clear to me. Then, shame, guilt, and condemnation came into my life.

The physical affection we shared was purely lust and based on deception. But as a needy person, at this point in my life, it met my yearning to feel significant and of value. The deception I was under provoked me to believe that I was special to the pastor and that he really needed me. However, as I later discovered, he was driven by his physical and emotional desires, and I merely served as a conduit for them. In other words, I was not special to him, just available.

Often, I thought to myself, "What am I doing? And why? He is a married man, not your high school sweetheart! Worst yet, he is your pastor." The guilt began to pile upon me like a weight. I felt dirty. A cloud of heaviness moved in, and I felt myself literally connect with an unclean spirit. My body, once the temple of the

Holy Spirit (1 Corinthians 6:19), now represented utter defilement and uncleanness. I wanted out, yet I wanted to stay in. "This man needs me and I want to be there for him" became my way of thinking.

Each time we had physical contact, the darkness in my soul grew darker and the gaping hole of emptiness I felt inside increased. What I had been seeking all my life seemed to continue to elude me, to be so out of reach. I sought a romantic relationship with someone who would listen to my dreams and my goals. I yearned for someone to love and cherish me. In retrospect, I realize that Pastor was also obviously experiencing a lot of pain, and I was simply his first-aid kit. I was a pseudo pain reliever for him. He searched for, reached out for, and demanded more than I could ever possibly give.

So here we were, two needy people—a pastor and one of his sheep. Both of us, in dire need of a Savior, sought refuge from the storm, but in the wrong place, in the wrong way, and devoid of God's divine plan. How often we all turn to pseudo pain relievers for a quick fix, when all we have to do is turn to Jesus. No matter what the problem is for each one of us, the right answer awaits us through Jesus Christ, for His blood paid the ultimate price.

As I stated earlier, the pastor and I had our first physical encounter after he had visited me on several occasions. After the initial illicit liaison occurred, he asked me to drop the title of "Pastor" and call him by his first name. He joked about the fact that we were sleeping together, and I was yet calling him "Pastor." The ease with which this pastor approached our relationship was beyond me. Unfortunately, over the years his heart had grown very cold, and he appeared to have no inner conviction regarding his behavior. Seemingly unaffected, he appeared totally oblivious to the fact that we were actually having an affair and acted as though all was "normal."

I experienced an indescribable feeling of depravity and accompanying feelings of nausea after that first physical encounter with the pastor. After he left my apartment, I sat down to contemplate the gravity of my choice and my actions. What had I done? I felt sorrow and regret, but I also felt as though he might really love me. (How blind I was, for this was yet another deceptive thought planted by the Enemy.) In the spiritual realm, I began a rapid descent into a bottomless demonic abyss. Even when I wanted to do what was right and good, evil was ever present with me, and I became subject to its insistent demands (Romans 7:19–23). I blindly interpreted Pastor's advances as, "He needs me."

In prior counseling sessions, Pastor had told Fred and me that, to add excitement to his sex life, he would watch sex channels on the cable networks because it made him do "crazy things" and heightened his sex drive. He had insinuated that to view such channels—in the sanctity of one's bedroom—would add spice to our relationship. (Pastor never appeared to feel any conviction about viewing pornography, nor did it seem he perceived it as sinful activity. However, unknown to him, because of this activity, demonic strongholds were being established in the spiritual realm, and he was indeed a victim of them.)

Already, during our first year of marriage, Fred and I had engaged in viewing pornography on videos, in magazines, and in other literature. We, too, had become victims of its alluring, enticing grip. However, then I began attending church regularly. I felt convicted about viewing it, and, over time, I stopped. Yet, this pastor was endorsing it as being acceptable for married couples. "The bed is undefiled when you are married," was his justification, stretching Scripture beyond its clear original intent. Since pornography was already a stronghold in our lives, Pastor's endorsement of it encouraged us to keep this particular "sin pattern" active in our marriage. At that time in my immature walk with God, I did not have the revelation that pornography is a stronghold. I had not been involved in a church that imparted such teaching. In fact, I had never heard anyone minister or preach on the specific types of "strongholds." However, inwardly, I felt it was wrong and would come under conviction when viewing it.

In later years, I learned through the teaching of God's Word that those who walk according to the flesh will fulfill the lust of the flesh and will forsake "all" for just one opportunity of fleeting pleasure. It was this same spirit of lust, this very same stronghold, that guided Pastor and me to forsake our relationships with God to pursue quick, forbidden encounters.

In addition, Pastor disclosed to me that he suffered from haunting childhood issues. He had been born illegitimately as a product of an unfortunate, perverted relationship. Furthermore, a background of homosexuality, infidelity, and pornography only exacerbated the emotional baggage that he silently carried. Despite these grievous problems, this wounded man acknowledged the call on his life to be God's oracle. However, the Enemy had deceptively stepped in to rob him of this call.

Also, at that time, I did not understand the concept of "soul-ties." This term means literally "giving away a piece of one's soul." Soul-ties are ungodly spiritual attachments to another person. They are sexual or emotional connections through crushes and fantasies; through illicit involvement with boyfriends or girlfriends, ex-spouses, or pastors; or through any other ungodly and inappropriate connections.

But, later, as I progressed in a true Christian walk and my understanding of this concept, I discovered that all the people Pastor had ever slept with were now tied to my soul—as mine was to his: a transference of souls. I was getting deeper and deeper into a tangled web of spirits from which only God could deliver me. However, at the time, I did not realize this was happening. I just wanted to be a comforter for Pastor. I felt that he needed me and I needed him, and so I used this rationale to justify my sinful actions.

Pastor began calling me at night so he could either arrange to stop by or request that I meet him at a specific place. He insisted that I find a babysitter so that he could see me often. It appeared that he was increasingly becoming emotionally and physically attached to me. He wanted to be around me all the time. Conversely, his emotional attachment fed a need in me to be wanted as a woman. He called me several times a day to see how I was doing. He purchased gifts for me, expensive gifts that I could never have afforded. The control of demonic spirits over my soul deepened, and I began to sell out—but not completely, because I never had any peace. Constantly, I would wrestle with guilt and shame. I could never really justify my actions or motives because I knew I was wrong.

On the other hand, I could never understand the carefree attitude of Pastor. He was always happy to see me. He would whistle, sing, and share details about upcoming church services and his plans for church growth. It was as if we were walking in unity as husband and wife. My soul yearned to be needed, to be important, to be included. The pastor met that need as he sought my advice and discussed with me the details of "church business." I could never quite grasp or understand his casual approach to our affair. Maybe it was because I was not his first mistress, and none of this was new to him. I had never before been involved with a married man, and worse yet, with a pastor; therefore, I was not prepared for the constant deceit, scheming, and lying that had to be incorporated into my day-to-day activities in order for meetings and schedules to be planned, arranged, and rearranged. There is no way I can describe the knot that stayed in my stomach because of my newly acquired lifestyle. Yet, it was all I had, and so I just kept holding on.

We would sometimes meet at hotels during the day. We would actually go to hotels in the city in which we both resided. I was always a nervous wreck regarding the deception and the sneaking around. Yet, Pastor made light of it and appeared to see each rendezvous as another opportunity to demonstrate his inability to get caught. (The Enemy wants sin to be exciting, risky, fun, daring—and then he crashes in on your parade and laughs at your flagrant stupidity.) Pastor's philosophy was that if we met at a local public spot, we would avoid rumors. He stated that rumors are started when you appear to be sneaking around. He believed that if you were bold about it, people wouldn't question it. Therefore, he believed that to be as conspicuous as possible would distract attention. Baffled, I would then ask him, "If they see us coming out of a hotel together, or even see our cars parked at a hotel, won't that be a clue?" He answered assuredly, "Unless they catch us in the act, they can't prove anything." I remained in awe of Pastor's ability to staunchly uphold his point of view and remain in control of any situation.

Throughout our affair, I continued to attend Pastor's church, where I would listen to him preach God's Word. I asked him on several occasions, "How can you preach God's Word and yet have an affair with me? Aren't you afraid? Don't you feel guilty?" He would patiently respond by telling me that God knew he was a man and that men have needs. He told me God also knew how unhappy he was with his wife, and that God wanted him to be happy. He explained to me that God doesn't sit up in the sky with a big hammer ready to bang us on the head just because we sin. Rather, he assured me that God loved both of us and He understood our need to be loved.

I clearly remember thinking, after hearing his justification regarding our sinful actions, that this answer was worse than the reply he gave for being conspicuous when we went to local hotels.

Sometimes, when I was at home, I would sit in silence and contemplate what I was doing, and I would just shake my head in disbelief. Darkness was closing in on me, and I knew it.

I Gave It All Away
(But He Was Still Reaching for Me)

God gave it all to me,
Expecting not a thing
in return.
I gave it all away,
Forsook all for nothing
in return.
God saw my broken heart,
Still reaching out to me
to return.

All I had to do was trust Him.
He asked little of me, from me.
I cried — He wanted to hold me.
To Pastor's arms I went instead.

Though God had answers for my life,
I searched for my own destiny.
He saw my mistaken pathway,
and still He wanted to hold me.

I knew my Lord once face-to-face.
I was drawing closer to Him.
But then I pulled away instead,
And followed the voice of the Deceiver.

I wept; He wept along with me.
He reached for me, I turned away.
"Just look at me," I said, downcast.
"There's nothing left to give to You."

Still He reached out His arms to me
To pull me close to His pure heart.
He still wanted to hold me close?
I drew back — "Not now, I can't!"

"Just look at me!" I said to Him.
He looked at me with eyes of love.
I felt His gaze search through my heart.
"Go away, please—I'm not worthy!"

I turned aside once more to leave,
And yet, when I looked back at Him
He was still reaching out for me.
With open arms reaching for me
to return.

Chapter Five

The Meeting

One evening, after an encounter with Pastor, and approximately forty-five minutes after he left my house, the phone rang. I heard his voice when I picked up the receiver. He told me that he was home in bed, but that his wife was not there. He expressed suspicion that she might be looking for him and heaved a sigh of relief that he had left my home when he did. Just as I mentioned my hope that she wouldn't come over to my house, I heard a knock at my door.

I spoke into the receiver to Pastor, "Someone is at my door." Pastor instructed me, "Answer the door; I will stay on the line." I laid the phone down on my bed and went to answer the knock. It was Pastor's wife. I numbly opened the door. Pastor's wife asked if her husband was there.

"No," I told her. She asked to come in. I let her in. She looked around and then looked at me. She asked if Pastor had been in my home. "No," I lied. Awkwardly, I offered her a seat. She then sat down at my kitchen table, and I sat across from her. She looked me in the eyes and asked me point-blank, "Are you having an affair with my husband?" "No," I again lied. She then confessed to me that she felt Pastor was interested in me.

As she continued to talk to me, I found myself staring into the hurt in her sad eyes as they pierced mine from across my table. I will never forget looking at the wife of this pastor, nor will I ever forget her almost grievous accusation, in the form of an inquiry, "Are you having an affair with my husband?" That question silently stabbed at my heart. It was the most degrading, humiliating thing I had ever been asked—yet I deserved every question she hurled at me, for I alone had disgraced and debased myself by my lurid lifestyle and wrong choices. Her heart was broken and her sorrow overwhelming. I was to blame. I was the "other woman."

All of a sudden, it became all too clear to me why she was withdrawn, why she avoided women. Whom could she trust? I had known her for several years, and now I, too, had "stabbed" her. Once again, this pastor's wife was experiencing betrayal, a feeling that I believe she knew all too well.

I will never forget her sad eyes as she looked straight into mine during our conversation. Oh, how I wanted to turn away or hold my head down in shame, but I did not. Instead, I looked straight at her as I silently fought back the tears. The pain within her was so obvious. Most distressing of all was that I knew I was responsible for her breaking heart.

But she never cried; she just painfully returned my gaze. She remained calm, though I knew she was crushed, her burden seemingly too immense, too heavy to carry any further.

As I looked at her, I wondered how many times she had traveled this road. I thought of how she had had to humble herself to knock on my door to ask if her own husband was at another woman's house. She got up after saying a few more words and started toward the door. She turned to me and said, "If he comes over here, tell him I am looking for him." I nodded my head. Then she left. I knew that she knew.

After I closed the door behind her stooped, departing frame, I went back to my bedroom where I picked up the phone. Almost numb from the experience, I whispered, still in a daze, "It was your wife; she just left."

Pastor wanted to know what was said. I told him we would talk about it later and that I had to go. Overcome with shame, I hung up the phone.

There are no words that I can use to describe the sickening dismay and inner pain and grief I experienced from that meeting with Pastor's wife. "What have I become?" I thought. "How could I sleep with Pastor, attend his church, and then sit across from his wife and boldly lie? God have mercy on my wretched soul! Who am I? I used to be a Christian woman who had earned the respect of others. I knew God and the power of His resurrection."

I used to experience His presence, but now His presence could not be felt; it could not be found. I felt so all alone. All I could do was just put my face in my hands. I felt sick, sick, sick, sick. I wanted that pastor's wife to reach out to me, to hold me as I begged her for forgiveness. I wanted to cry and tell her, "I am so sorry." I wanted to confess to her what I had done. I was *so ashamed.* She had been in search of her husband—the pastor—at my house! "God help me," I thought.

That night, something began to change in me. I knew that somehow I had to get out of this relationship in spite of what Pastor said or felt. As I sat there thinking of how to tell him, my mind traveled back to our numerous talks. I had previously mentioned to Pastor that we had to end our affair. But Pastor had declared emphatically that he wouldn't be able to make it if I left him. He was so convincing, and he always made me feel guilty, as though I were betraying him by even making the suggestion.

As I sat there all alone in my living room that night, I groped for answers. I reflected on what he had been telling me: "Pat, I have no one but you. You are the only one who understands me. I love you, Pat." When I had persisted saying that we needed to end our affair, Pastor would become irritable. I would sometimes cry, and he would simply retort, "The next time I get a girlfriend, she is not going to be in the church. You keep whining about what God is thinking. God loves you, Pat. He loves me. He understands!"

I even remember responding, "The next time? You mean you would do this again?" He responded with a sarcastic chuckle, and then he told me he was unhappy with his wife and he needed someone whom he could love. Consequently, our conversations always ended with his saying how much he needed me and that he couldn't bear to lose me.

As I sat there and thought about my destructive situation, I finally surmised that I must be strong and courageous. I convinced myself to quit talking about all that I needed to do and to start acting on what I knew was right. In spite of my positive self-talk, I felt like I was in quicksand; the more I struggled to get out, the deeper I sank.

When we are in situations in which we feel all alone and hopeless, the Enemy will try to capitalize on our despair. In these times, it is easy for us to feel as if God cannot be reached and that He does not hear us because of the great sin in our lives. But I can tell you assuredly that God does see our struggles and hears our inward cries for help. We can come to a point in life when circumstances seem so overwhelming that we feel totally alone, without one person who understands, but God is there for us.

The self-imposed pressures caused by wrong decisions can seemingly dictate our destiny—unless God intervenes. He has a purpose and a plan for our lives that He wants to fulfill. So He stands ready at the opportunity to come to our rescue. He waits patiently for us to call to Him, to acknowledge our need for Him in our lives. If you so much as whimper and call God's name in the weakest of tones, He hears, and He is moved with compassion.

That night, after Pastor's wife had left my home, I whimpered. I was overcome with shame and had reached my lowest ebb in life. My soul yearned to be free, and my spirit yearned to be under the shadow of the Almighty; I longed for a place of refuge from the storm. I needed a hiding place. I needed my heavenly Father.

If Pastor's wife should ever read this book, I hope she will recognize the familiarity of this story and know that it is I, Patricia, who writes. To her, I say,

> I am deeply sorry for the pain and the hurt that I brought into your life. I know such words as "sorry" must seem so shallow in light of the agony you had to endure. Please know that for twelve years I walked under a veil of shame. I punished myself over and over again for the hurt that I caused you and for the pain that I saw in your eyes. For years, my past failure played in my mind as a constant, nagging memory, as if it were in automatic replay. I ask that you find it in your heart to forgive me, if you have not already. I desire to personally apologize to you for the needless pain you bore as a result of my thoughtless actions. But I dare not presume that such a request would be welcomed by you. I hurt you immensely, and I betrayed your trust. I will never forget your courage and the humility it must have taken

to come to my house in search of your husband that night.

May this apology I humbly extend to you be accepted. May it bring peace and not sorrow, closure and not an open door for the Enemy. I desire your forgiveness and your prayers as I seek to help others walk out of their individual prisons of shame.

God bless you and keep you in His peace.

I believe God will use my testimony to bring restoration and restitution to many who read this book—the women whose heads are hanging down in shame because they have had affairs, the pastors who have walked in this pastor's shoes, and the pastors' wives who have endured the hardships and pain of betrayal. In sincere repentance, I have gone to the Father and reckoned with Him regarding my iniquity, and He has forgiven me. His blood redeemed me and brought purity to my life.

From the standpoint of restitution and restoration, the Enemy will pay for the damages: he will observe women and men, nationally and internationally, walk out of their chains of bondage. His plan to thwart the call of God on their lives by holding them captive to their shame will be used against him as women and men declare their freedom through their spoken testimonies. Thus, their declarations will release others to become free. As they determine in their spirits that they will not continue in the path of the downcast, but rather the uplifted, and as they boldly tell their stories, these will become contagious acts of courage. They will walk under a veil of glory as God's everlasting mercy is communicated through them to others, and restoration will be imminent for the fallen man and woman. I believe these things to be so by the power of God.

The Meeting

You knocked on my door, and I let you in.
You knew it was here your husband had been.
My heart was so heavy and filled with shame.
You questioned motives; I denied the same.

You sat at my table, across from me
As I gazed at you in my misery.
Here you sat, his wounded and betrayed wife,
Whom I had known many years of my life.

Your eyes so sad, your posture bent and worn,
Your heavy heart burdened; your look, forlorn.
"Dear God," I cried silently, "what've I done?"
To my own home this poor woman has come
In search of her husband, to find her spouse
Who seconds before, left my bed, my house.

I answered you with evasions and lies.
Outwardly I endured, inwardly cried.
You were betrayed by him and now by me,
I, a part of the web, you too, us three.
And the ones who were connected before—
Were soul-tied with us, by the opened door.

You rose to go, started to leave my house;
Then you said, "Give this message to my spouse.
Tell him that I have been looking for him,"
For you knew my home was where he had been.
"Okay," I said, and I bent down my head,
My heart was pounding and filled with dread.

I thought to myself as I looked at you,
What more could I say, what more could I do?
That night I sat alone and wept out loud,
"Dear God, can You turn this nightmare around?

"I need You right now, won't You please help me?
I've got to get out, escape, and be free."
Resolve took over; I made up my mind
I would tell Pastor the very next time
That it is over, for once and for all,
Do not come again; do not ever call.

Section Two:
God's Grace

Chapter Six

The Quandary

I had previously written about Pastor and our affair to my older sister, Sherrie. I had been in possession of her reply for a week or so. As I read it over, I sensed that her concern over the situation reflected urgency. She insisted that I leave immediately, without hesitation. She told me that I must find another church.

After reading her letter, I was even more convinced that I had to leave. It had only been a few days since Pastor's wife had visited my home. I was trying to plan an escape, and I rehearsed what I would say. This pastor was very persuasive, and I was afraid he would talk me into staying. I kept telling myself to be strong and to stick to my commitment to leave. When the Pastor stopped by after work, I told him that I had to leave, that I could no longer deal with our illicit relationship. I told him that the confrontation with his wife was more than I could bear and that I was utterly ashamed.

The pastor began to sob. He got on his knees, held my hands, and begged me not to leave. He literally cried and cried. He told me he would have no one if I left. He kept telling me that he needed me and to please not leave him. I argued with him and told him he was being unfair to me. I told him I needed to get my life right with God again. He asked me where I would go, and I told him I had heard of a church that was in another city. I told him I would go there. "No, no, don't leave me!" he cried. "Please let me go!" I cried back. "I love you, Pat," he said. "I need you. Please don't leave me. I have no one else but you." Pierced by his outcries of helplessness, I relented and stayed.

It seemed as if an eternity went by after the day I made the decision to stay. Time slowly passed, until our affair reached the fourth month. It felt more like it had been four years of my life. Each day was long and burdensome. Sadness and despondency became my constant companions. How I wanted to be free and make a fresh start. I moved into a new apartment, and my mother flew in from out of state to assist me with the unpacking.

Since my mother was an ordained evangelist, Pastor invited her to speak at his church. My mother knew Pastor and his wife on an acquaintance basis. Initially, Mom had met Pastor when she had visited my former husband and me several years earlier. At that time, Pastor had overseen another congregation in another city in which we all resided. Also, on one other occasion, Pastor had visited my parents at their home.

Unaware of our affair, Mom accepted Pastor's invitation to preach at his church. Her message, "I Am Satisfied with Jesus, but Is Jesus Satisfied with Me?" ripped at my soul. I was utterly ashamed and embarrassed. By now there were whispers at the church that I was involved with the pastor. And here in the church stood my own mother who preached a message that tore through to the core of my very being. I wanted desperately to yell out, "No, Jesus is not satisfied with me!" I sat in the back of the church and wept as she preached. I did not want anyone to look at me or to focus in my direction. I was drowning, and there was no apparent lifeline, no one who could help me.

I had no established relationships with any of the ladies from church. The one to whom I felt the closest was still far too distant for me to confide in for help. Though the pastor and I had never been caught in the act, the word was out. We were clearly under suspicion.

I desperately needed a lifeline. It was as if I were dangling by a thread. I felt hopeless. I wanted to tell my mother, but how could I bring myself to mouth such a sordid confession? I struggled with telling her, but every time I got the courage to, I would change my mind.

During the two weeks my mother visited me, Pastor stopped by only once "to see my mother," or so it appeared. He did not call me or request a meeting. During this time, I prayed and asked

God for help to leave him. I got up enough courage to tell my mother that I was "infatuated" with the pastor. I asked her to pray for me. She did. She hugged me and told me that I was just lonely, and she assured me that God had someone special for me. She didn't scowl at me for the "infatuation story" at all. I almost felt I could tell her the truth, but then I again changed my mind. Mom departed to return home. I was left alone again.

Pastor called later on that day to tell me he was coming over. My kids were in day care, and I did not have any classes or work that day. (I was a full-time college student and a part-time employee.) I told him on the phone that I wanted to end it and not to come over. He insisted, "I'm coming over." He was at my door within the hour. Again, another encounter took place. I cried, "I can't go on like this. My mother just preached a message about whether God was satisfied with me. He's not." Pastor refused to listen and kept reminding me of his need for me.

He eventually left. I sat in my bedroom, which had now become a "defiled den of iniquity." This had been Pastor's first time alone with me in my apartment since I had moved in. I had wanted to keep the environment pure, but now the evil spirits were running rampant in my new apartment.

I began to cry like never before. I sobbed and sobbed before the Lord. "Help me!" I cried out. "This is bigger than me, and I do not have the power to fight it." Satan was holding me in captivity. He knew I was too weak to stand up to the pastor. Only God could break the chains of Satan's control in my life.

Everything within me was crushed. I felt as if I were literally on the brink of falling apart. My heart was broken, my spirit was limp, and I was barely hanging on. My body, soul, and spirit, though defiled, were desperately pleading for mercy. I gasped as though my heart would break as I fell on my knees and face and came before His mercy seat. With everything within me, I desperately cried out for help.

Over and over again, I asked for God's forgiveness. I had sinned against Him, the body of Christ, my family, and myself. The shame of my sins was before me and upon me. I repented and repented and repented and cried and wailed. I cried so hard that my stomach ached. Then, suddenly, as if I had been given a tranquilizer, I fell into a deep, deep sleep for about two hours. When I awoke, all I could remember was dreaming about angels walking around me. I sat there for a few minutes as I gathered my thoughts. I then glanced at my watch. I was startled at the time. I had to rush to get my children from day care.

Just as I was getting ready to leave, the phone rang. It was Pastor. Suddenly, a new courage and strength rose up in me. Without wincing or batting an eye, I told him it was over! I would never be back to his church. I told him I had been forgiven and that I was going to get back on the right track with God. I informed him that I would be joining another church in another city.

He then did the usual begging and crying for me to stay. I made it clear once again that it was over, and then I hung up on him. The phone rang again. It was Pastor. I hung up. The phone rang several times, and I picked it up and immediately hung up again. It felt good to finally put the Devil under my feet. He had been riding my back for too long, and I was glad I was finally throwing him off.

I no longer felt any emotional ties with Pastor whatsoever. It was absolutely amazing! A complete transformation had taken place as I slept. I had an inexplicable strength that was supernaturally imparted. I knew I wasn't going to change my mind. God had broken the chains and set me free!

I believe in my spirit that, while I slept, the angels I had dreamed of were actually dispatched by God to fight the battle I could not fight. They destroyed the Enemy and overtook the powers of darkness. My Father in heaven heard my cry, and He delivered me! I was freed from the stronghold of Satan and his dominion and control in my life. His grip had been broken! I was coming home to God. All my heavy burdens were noticeably gone. I was happy and free as I departed to pick up my children.

Chapter Seven

The Prodigal Daughter

I will never forget the day I walked into the crowded church. I had never seen such a boisterous display of jubilant worship. People unashamedly stood in the foyer of this church and boldly prayed. On one side, I saw men holding hands with men, and women with women, in prayer. In another corner, I saw two women and one man holding hands and praying. At the other end, I saw a man and a woman praying for one another. Rejoicing, people cried to each other, "Be blessed" and, "God is awesome."

In a daze, I slowly absorbed this unabashed, unpretentious scene as I walked around the corner into the sanctuary. There, I found a seat in the back of the packed sanctuary with my two little children. It had been one week since I had broken emotional and physical ties with Pastor.

How I yearned to be in the presence of the Lord where no one would look at me or scorn me. Though it was a bit overwhelming, it felt so good to be in this church. I sensed such love and authenticity among these people.

They sang songs with an oompah, Jewish beat. I had never heard songs like these before. In the front of the sanctuary, identically dressed ladies with ribbons tied to their tambourines skillfully waved their instruments with exhilaration and unbridled joy.

There were so many young people in this church who were my age. There were as many men as there were women. I found that to be quite unusual. These young people earnestly danced before the Lord with all their might. I knew I had found my home. This was where I would take refuge from the storm and begin my healing. And, oh, how I wanted to be healed of the huge, gaping wounds that I bore, yet no one else could see. I knew that if there were ever a place to begin my healing, it was this church, Christian House of Prayer. I had heard good things about the pastor and his wife and how they really loved God and His people. I did not know the pastor's name yet, but I was so excited to be in the midst of this great congregation. I was overwhelmingly grateful to God for directing me there.

After a time of heartfelt worship, the pastor rose to speak. He was one of the most radiant men I had ever seen. He smiled and greeted the people with a hearty "Amen" and "Praises to God." I turned to the person next to me and asked the name of the pastor. "His name is Pastor Nate Holcomb, and his wife is Pastor Valerie," was the reply. (During the writing of this book, I discovered that Pastor Holcomb is now a bishop—a promotion from God!)

Pastor Holcomb began to lead the church in a confession of faith that went something like this: "People are standing in line to get into this church to hear the Word of God. For this is a prosperous year for us, and the doors of success have been opened. We shall succeed in everything through Christ. The door of failure has been closed, and we shall not know defeat." They repeated this three times, and then they closed with Romans 4:21: "*And being fully persuaded that, what he ha[s] promised, he [is] able also to perform*" (KJV).

Oh, how desperately I wanted to confess what they were saying. I wanted to confess that I would not know defeat any more in my life. "I am going to learn that confession," I thought to myself. I felt as if I were in heaven. "Thank you, God, for sending me here! These people really believe in you, Lord! I believe they must really love You."

Then, at the conclusion of his message, I heard the pastor say, "Maybe we have a prodigal daughter or a prodigal son who wants to come home. This is your day. Don't put it off any longer.

"You knew the Lord, but you turned your back on Him," he continued. "You left home and ended up in the pigpen of life, but you've come to your senses, and now you want to come home. Your Father is waiting for you. He wants to put a ring on your finger and throw a robe around you as He welcomes you home.

He's preparing a celebration for your homecoming. Are you ready to come home?"

By this time, I was crying so hard, I couldn't see. My little girl kept asking me if I was okay. "Yes, sweetie, I'm fine," I told her. Amid my heart-wrenching sobs, I got up and went down the aisle to the front of the church. I honestly don't know if anyone else answered the altar call that day because, as far as I knew, it was just me and the Lord. I had come home!

I actually sensed that He was waiting for me, to place a robe around me and a ring on my finger. And what a glorious homecoming He had arranged for me at the altar that Sunday morning. "I'll never leave you again, Father; I will never leave you again," I cried out, with my arms extended to the heavens and hot tears of joy streaming down my cheeks. "I'm home, dear Father—I'm finally home!"

As Pastor Holcomb prayed for me, and as others gathered and laid hands on me, the Lord met me that day at the altar. I was gloriously baptized with the Holy Spirit. I literally felt my Father's arms around me. He held me like a baby as I cried and rejoiced.

"I'm home and I'm free!" I proclaimed. I had found my way back home to God and was free from my relationship with Pastor and the strongholds of sin. I felt like Martin Luther King, Jr., that day. "Free at last, free at last, thank God Almighty, I am free at last!"

The Prodigal's Heart

Like a husband He was to me,
Looking after my cares, my needs.
His provision in my life was seen.
By faith I walked, in Him was clean.

But as the world turned, so did I,
for I departed and left His side.
I sought to fill my flesh with sin—
absorbed it all and took it in.

While on my journey, life seemed unfair;
I was so lonely and in despair.
Where was the joy I had known before?
The peace? The grace? and so much more?

Would He be happy if I came home?
I miss my Beloved, I'm so alone.
He always promised that He'd be there,
no matter what, no matter where.

I journeyed home; I hoped to see
That, like a husband, He'd be waiting for me.
As I crossed the threshold, there He stood,
Waiting for my arrival as I'd hoped He would.

As our eyes met, the tears came, too.
The faster we ran, the closer we drew.
He picked me up and spun me around,
And on my head He placed a crown.

"My princess, you have come home to Me;
I missed your face, your praise, your glee."
He loved me and He held me close,
I loved Him so, but He loved me most.

What grace, what mercy, He had for me!
No questions asked, no hesitancy.
He took me back just as I was,
And gave me His unbridled love.

To His presence I had flown,
He embraced me as I had never known.
"Welcome home," He whispered to me,
"I stood in the gap so this could be.
And now you're home, don't ever flee,
for in Me lies your destiny."

I knelt on the ground and washed His feet.
I wept at His throne, His mercy seat.
My alabaster box was at my side;
He knew my thoughts, and He wiped my eyes.

As I reached for it, He touched my hand.
"You are forgiven, Patricia Ann."
What manner of love might this be,
that He would say such things to me?

His love so pure, His commitment strong,
forever with Him I do belong.
"From this day forth, will you be My bride
And never again leave My side?"
He asked of me with tears in His eyes.
"I will," I said, finally wise.

Then on my finger He placed His ring,
A beautiful gem from my Beloved, the King.
And on my shoulders He placed His robe,
and to each other we were betrothed.

Chapter Eight

God's Princess

With every Bible study, praise and worship service, or fellowship gathering, God drew my heart closer to my new church family. My children made new friends, and I experienced restoration, joy, and peace.

At long last, my life took on new purpose and significance as I pursued my college studies while working in an Equal Employment Opportunity (EEO) branch office of the civil service. My boss, a strong, vibrant woman of Baptist background, staunchly believed it was important to reach out and help others achieve, and she lived it in her everyday actions.

My boss came into my office early one morning and told me that a city pageant was to be held and that she would like me to become a contestant. She said the participants would be judged on talent, creativity, appearance, fitness, and personality. I explained to her that I possessed none of the above.

She encouraged me, however. "I will teach you how to do a dramatization," she replied, undaunted. She introduced me to the works of James Weldon Johnson, including his great poetic piece entitled "The Creation." This eloquent verse describes the creation of man by God. She instructed me to memorize the words. She would then work with me at the end of each day and teach me the dramatic gestures.

Unable to find any more excuses, I entered the contest. A friend agreed to watch my children for a few days after work so I could make the practices. I practiced every night at home on "The Creation" until I knew every word and every move without thinking or blinking an eye.

One day, while I was at work, a young lady named Joann, who also attended Christian House of Prayer, came in to interview for a position at the EEO office. She was offered the job and began working shortly thereafter. I shared with Joann my excitement about the upcoming pageant. I told her that one of the pageant requirements was that each participant have a male escort, and I explained that I had no one to ask. She emphatically stated, "I know just the guy." She said that he was single and good looking. "He is very nice. I bet he would be glad to escort you," Joann said. I asked her if she would find out, and she said she would. The next day, at work, she told me he said he would be glad to escort me. I was scheduled to meet him at church on Wednesday before the evening service. I was told he was a musician and would be involved in a pre-service rehearsal. "Look for the guy on the drums," Joann said. "His name is Eddie Harris."

I met Eddie on that Wednesday night. Though we only had a brief introduction, I knew he was a kind man with a gentle nature. He was well groomed and pleasant; his demeanor was that of a gentleman. Inwardly, I thanked God that Joann had thought of Eddie to be my escort.

During each rehearsal, Eddie would come at the appointed time for his part in the pageant and would leave directly afterward. Eddie was the perfect gentleman. At the close of each practice, he said a few encouraging words and told me he would see me at the next rehearsal. He carried himself in a manner without question. Eddie never flirted, and he treated me with the utmost respect. I liked his qualities; they were rare to me, yet authentic. I remember wistfully thinking, "Perhaps he will ask me out for ice cream or a burger one of these evenings after rehearsal." But he never did, and I never hinted at my interest in him. I had made up my mind that God would go before me in all that I did and said. But I expressed to God, "I like Eddie—very much."

The night of the pageant came, and Eddie was right there by my side. He escorted me on my walk as they introduced me. I was so nervous! But Eddie told me that it would be okay, and he continued to encourage me through each phase of the pageant.

Before I knew it, it was time for the contestants to perform in the talent competition. Eddie said a prayer and assured me that I would do fine. He was right. I received a standing ovation that lasted for what seemed like forever. The audience so enthusiastically thundered their applause that I was both speechless and overwhelmed. It was unbelievable! Though I had never performed a dramatic presentation before in my life, that night God anointed my talent. As I stood there, the continuous applause from the audience made me feel like a million dollars.

It was finally time to call the top five runners-up. My name was called along with the other four. I was so excited! From this point, the pageant progressed to the awards for the various segments. I can still remember the awards as if it were yesterday. They were:

Category 1:   Most Creative (This segment consisted of a narrative written by each contestant, describing her goals and daily lifestyle. These narratives were read by each contestant, in turn, as another contestant walked and modeled her sports outfit.)

Category 2:   Most Talented (This consisted of a selected talent presented for competition.)

Category 3:   Ms. Congeniality

Crowning: Ms. Princess (The chosen princess for the 1987 pageant)

The spokesperson called out, "And the Most Creative award goes to...Patricia Weaver." Eddie, who was standing next to me onstage, winked at me as I went out to accept my trophy. Again, I received a standing ovation.

The pageant's emcee turned to face the audience again, and continued, "And the Most Talented award goes to...Patricia Weaver!" I looked up at Eddie, and again he beamed with genuine happiness at my unforeseen double blessing. I stepped out once more to accept the award, my heart bursting with joy. That night, I truly felt as if I were the recipient of two Grammy awards.

The Ms. Congeniality award was then given to one of the most amiable young ladies I have ever met.

As the emcee came to the conclusion of the evening's festivities, Eddie looked at me and said, "I believe it is you. I believe you are going to win the crown." Shortly after he said those words, the pageant host paused for a moment. Then, with the card identifying the winner in her hand, she spoke in a high, resonant voice that pierced the hushed auditorium: "Our first runner up is..." When she didn't call my name, I knew I had won the title. "And our new Princess for 1987 is...Ms. Patricia Weaver!"

"Oh, my God," I said to myself in wide-eyed disbelief and shock. As I numbly walked to center stage and received my beautiful silver rhinestone tiara, a satin sash, and bouquet of roses, I thought, "Can this be true?" That night, I was crowned a "Princess" before hundreds of people who applauded my success. As the music played, I walked onto the runway with Eddie, my escort, by my side, waving through tearful eyes to the cheering crowd. Eddie then stood aside and let me walk alone. As I took my victory walk, though outwardly smiling and waving at the well-wishers, I inwardly thought about where I had come from just a few months ago. In that not-too-distant past, I had wallowed in the pigpen. But, tonight, I had been given a new name, a new identity, and a crown, all because of God's awesome love. I deserved nothing, yet He gave me everything. He wanted me to know that He saw me as His princess.

I am reminded of a woman who was crowned a national princess many years ago. Shortly after her victory, it was discovered that her past consisted of questionable behavior that did not bring honor to the crown. This precious soul was stripped of her glory and the accolades. The media discredited her and cast shame upon her. No longer was she viewed a "princess" in their eyes. They took her crown away for failure to meet pageant criteria. She was perceived as unworthy to be a princess, according to the rules.

Yet, here I stood, amid resounding applause, the least of all. Every woman in the pageant was worthier than I. My past was made plain before God; He knew my failures, my track record of impurity. And yet, He allowed me to be crowned a princess. This pageant was a manmade event, but I believe God was the ultimate judge. Just as God chose David, who was out in the field tending the sheep and was considered to be the least of all, He also chose me. I was the least likely to be worthy of a crown, but God, who knew my unspeakable failures and the shame of my past, viewed me as His princess. He bypassed the usual "rules" and counted me worthy. He pronounced me a princess and gave me a crown.

My Father God knew how little I thought of myself and how I struggled with personal shame. So, in His own special way, He lifted my chin and held my head up. In His eyes, I was somebody special. I was not rejected, but was *"accepted in the Beloved"* (Ephesians 1:6) through Christ Jesus.

"Thank you, sweet Jesus," I said as I continued to wave to the cheering crowd and walk the length of the stage. I completed my walk and went back to stand beside Eddie. He looked at me and said what my own heart was feeling, "Praise God!"

God's Princess

How could I be a princess,
with a crown, awards, and gifts?
I feel so unworthy.

Yet God said, "I count you worthy,
My ways are past finding out.
As far as the east is from the west,
so are your sins from Me," He said.
"I have cast them into the sea of forgetfulness
to remember them no more.
I will have mercy upon whom I will have mercy.
Though your sins be as scarlet,
I will wash them whiter than snow.
Come to the mercy seat and experience
My grace, My love.
I am great and greatly to be praised, for I alone reign.
My purpose will always prevail.
All have fallen short of My glory.
Yet, all can obtain right standing because of My grace,
because of the redemptive blood of Jesus.
Tell them that I AM crowned you
and made you a princess."

Chapter Nine

My Knight in Shining Armor

As the newly crowned City Princess, I was scheduled to make guest appearances at luncheons, banquets, modeling shows, churches, breakfasts, recreation centers, and wherever they could send me. I was asked to perform "The Creation" at most of my guest appearances. Eddie was asked by the pageant officials to be present at every appearance to serve as my escort. Eddie kindly acquiesced, freely volunteering his services. To me, I felt he was a protector sent by God Himself.

After one month of guest appearances, the friendship between Eddie and me began to blossom. As our interest in one another developed into a romantic attraction, Eddie asked me out on a date. We went bowling, taking my children on our first date. The following week, we went on a picnic with the children. On our third date, we went to a drive-in movie with my two little buddies in tow. After these three dates, Eddie felt that the Lord had told him that I was to be his wife. He asked me to marry him. My mouth almost fell open. I didn't expect a proposal from Eddie. I had never experienced such genuine love, gentleness, and kindness as had been shown to me by this man. We had dated only three times and known each other for just a few months. Despite this, I knew Eddie was genuine and sincere, totally different from any man I had ever known. When I was with Eddie, I forgot my sordid past. It was as if I had crossed over into another world—an innocent, pure world.

I said yes to his proposal without even thinking about all that I needed to disclose to him. I was so excited and happy. "Yes, yes, yes" was all I could think and say.

Within a week, the Lord impressed upon my heart to share my past with Eddie. Deep within, I had been agonizing over how to share it with him. I just didn't know what to expect. I was fearful of losing Eddie, yet I knew he had to know the truth about me and my past. The word from the Lord was to tell him soon, without delay. I submitted to God's direction.

Inwardly, I wrestled about how to share my deepest, darkest secrets with Eddie. Should I tell him I had genital herpes first, or should I tell him about my affair with Pastor? How awful it was going to be. I could only imagine the worst. I cried because I knew my past was who I was, and I could not run away from the truth. It had been almost a year since the beginning of the affair with the pastor. The painful memories were still there. I knew I had been forgiven, yet the shame from my past was overwhelming.

The following Sunday, Eddie invited my children and me over for dinner at his apartment after church. He was a very good cook and had prepared a delicious meal for us. After we ate, the kids lay down for a nap. I then told Eddie that I needed to discuss something with him. We stepped out into a field across from his apartment building. I could see the balcony door of Eddie's apartment from the field where I stood. He had left it open so that we could hear the kids if they awakened. It was warm that evening, and I remember seeing the stars twinkle brightly as nightfall rapidly approached.

Though I had now acquired a new name as a princess and many of the local townspeople referred to me by this title, I also had a past from which I could not escape. I felt I would be haunted by the stigma of my illicit relationship with Pastor for the rest of my life. I knew Eddie wanted and deserved a precious jewel for a wife, a woman of virtue. He deserved to have such, and I knew I was tainted. As I attempted to tell Eddie, I could not control the tears. In fact, I could barely speak.

Patiently, Eddie held me close and continued to tenderly inquire about what was bothering me. Finally, he gently urged, "Just say it, Patricia." I knew there was no easy way to say it. With all the courage I had, I relayed to Eddie about the herpes first—the lesser of the two evils, in my opinion. I explained how it had come about in my previous marriage. He looked at me and said, "Is that it?" (Is that it? I couldn't believe my ears. He didn't wince or grimace when I told him about my incurable sexually transmitted disease.) He told me we would deal with it together and make the best of the situation. Eddie assured me that herpes would not prevent us from getting married, nor did it change his love for me.

I told him there was more that I needed to share. As I looked into his eyes, with tears pouring down my cheeks, I confessed to this dear, unassuming young man that I had had a four-month affair with my previous pastor. I told him the name of the pastor. Eddie quietly acknowledged that he knew him. Eddie then looked at me with the most sincere eyes, held my chin in his hands, and unflinchingly stated, "If God has forgiven you, then so do I, Patricia, and you know that God has forgiven you. I love you, and I want you to be my wife." The matter was settled.

Then, out of the clear blue, Eddie picked me up and swung me around so as to lift my spirits and make me smile. He then stopped and held me like a baby, with my head against his chest and my ninety-eight-pound frame in his arms. He looked at me eye to eye and reassured me that we were supposed to be together. He said, "I love you, Patricia Harris." (He called me by his last name as a confirmation of his commitment to me, his bride-to-be.) He then put me down and hugged me like I was a china doll. We walked back to his apartment hand in hand. Tears of joy were streaming down my cheeks, for I knew God had given me the man of my dreams, the man I could share my hopes with, who would understand my needs and who would always be there. God had selected Eddie to be my husband, and me to be his wife.

As I look back on that night, I now realize that Eddie represented a type and shadow of God's unconditional love and His boundless mercy. God calls us by His name, no matter what our past may be. He picks us up and holds us like a baby, reassuring us of His love as He reminds us that we are His bride-to-be.

A few weeks after I disclosed my past to Eddie, he received a letter from a friend of his who told him that she had heard a rumor about me and felt he should know. This older lady was a dear friend and was only addressing the issue out of concern. She wanted to make sure that Eddie was aware of any possible hidden secrets. I believe that her heart was pure and that she was only looking out for his best interests. Eddie called this lady friend and informed her that we had already addressed the personal issues of my past, and he assured her that he knew, without a doubt, that I was the woman for him. I was so glad I had listened to the Lord about disclosing my past without delay. God knew that Eddie was soon to find out, and He wanted it to come from me first, before Eddie heard it from another.

Several ladies in the church whom I had come to know told me that Eddie had been at the church for more than two years, and that he was considered a "possible husband" for some of the single sisters. In other words, some of the young ladies were "naming and claiming," I guess. He was such a gentleman, very regal. I can certainly see why he was an eligible bachelor. Yet, God had reserved Eddie for me. He was my special blessing.

Three months after Eddie's proposal, we married. Eddie and I did not consummate our union until our wedding night. I was so happy! I was on the right path in life. I had overcome some odds in my life, and finally I could see the light at the end of the tunnel. I had a godly man for a husband, a man who really loved and cherished me, someone with whom I could share my dreams and secret ambitions, someone who believed in me. I loved my husband; I knew I would always love him and be a faithful wife. Eddie had a heart of gold. He was a real man, a man after God's own heart (1 Samuel 13:14).

The Knight in Shining Armor & His Princess

As a girl, I would dream of your great might.
You were a strong, valiant, and warring knight.
On your stallion you would ride into town;
people far and near would gather around.

Girls would dress pretty to catch your glances,
in hopes that their looks would help their chances.
And you were such a charming gentleman
That you would say kind words to all of them.

Yet in your search, you continued to ride,
Seeking high and low for a special bride.
Not just any young lady would be right,
But only a perfect match for this knight.

Who, then, is this special girl of your dreams?
You're seeking one who offers more, it seems.
The woman you want would truly love you
adore you, be faithful, and always be true.

Her trouble-filled past just would not prevent
All the love that to her you'd present.
You knew that some day you'd see her dear face,
Her shyness, her smile, and her godly grace.

Early one day you looked and there she stood,
standing on a path in the lovely wood.
She appeared so frail, yet she looked so sweet,
You knew this was the one you had to meet.

A gentleman, you offered her a ride
Upon your stallion, to sit by your side.
She looked up at you, and you gazed at her.
Could she be the real answer to your prayer?

Through many hours with this charming girl,
You noticed her smile, her eyes, and her curls.
She had found a true place within your heart;
    You couldn't leave her or be apart.

Then came the day when she confessed to you
Her hurts, her past, and all of her deep wounds.
You gently wiped her tears, you dried her eyes,
and you asked her if she would be your bride.

(The young girl speaks):
"When I was young, I dreamed of you.
I never thought it would come true.
All my life I've prayed for a man,
who would be true and understand,
That I've fallen short, and made mistakes,
and sometimes fallen on my face.
Can one accept me as I am?
I've asked God, 'Is there such a man?'"

(The knight speaks):
"I am he; yes, I am the one.
I understand from where you've come.
And I forgive you for your past.
Come, celebrate our love at last!"

They had a wedding to honor their life,
For he had completed the search for his wife.
They rode off together in happiness
For the knight had found his beautiful princess.

Chapter Ten

God's Amazing Grace

I n pursuit of Eddie's dream to play the drums professionally, we moved to Dallas two months after we were married. Due to the unanticipated move, I relinquished my crown as City Princess. So, in a formal ceremony, I passed the title on to the first runner-up. However, I knew that in God's eyes and in Eddie's, I would always be a princess. God had used the pageant to serve its purpose in my life, and I was content to move on. In the midst of this transition, I also discovered in our third month of marriage that I was pregnant. I was approximately four weeks along at the time we found out. Eddie was to become a first-time birth father.

At this point in our lives, all was going well. We both were adjusting to married life, Eddie for the first time and I for the second. As they say, the first year is always the toughest. Due to the fact that our courtship had been only three months in duration, Eddie and I learned about each other's peculiarities after we were married. We both were determined to adjust, and so we did. But to add to our period of adjustment, my herpes flared up three times in our first year of marriage. I was in my seventh month of pregnancy during the third flare-up. The doctor told me that if the herpes remained active at the time of the baby's delivery, I would have to undergo a caesarian section for the baby's protection.

Eddie never became upset about the herpes. He never seemed annoyed and never said a critical or cruel word to me regarding it. He refused to hurt or reject me in any way. Eddie was true to his word. He had said we would make the necessary adjustments, and we did. He was as calm about the herpes at the time of the flare-ups as he had been the night I confessed to him in the field by his apartment.

As the delivery day approached, Eddie and I discussed names for our new baby. I told Eddie that I was confident she was a girl. One day, while I was at home, cleaning, I paused and began to search the TV channels. I finally decided to stop momentarily at a channel that featured a talk show. As I continued my household cleaning, I suddenly heard the talk show host exclaim in astonishment, "Amazing grace!" At that same moment, I heard the Lord speak to my spirit and say, "Her name will be Amazing Grace." When Eddie came home from work, I told him what the Lord had said, but he had few words, if any, regarding the name. After all, Amazing Grace wasn't a name you would normally choose for your child.

So I asked God for a second confirmation, just so we could be sure. I felt, as Eddie himself admitted to me, that Amazing Grace was a very odd name for a child. One night, while the kids were in bed and Eddie was at work, I was in the den folding clothes and putting them away; again, I had the television on in the background. I was walking from the den to the bedroom and back again, methodically putting away clothes. As I did this, I heard the ending of a TV show, and the only words that caught my attention were "Amazing grace! Amazing grace!" I quickly walked over to the television and observed the credits as they rolled on the screen. There was an actor's name who played the role of "Amazing Grace." In this show, Amazing Grace was a boy. I took a seat, utterly shocked. I had never heard of anyone named Amazing Grace, boy or girl. This particular show was portraying the life of a baseball player. So God answered my prayer and confirmed the name. I shared the confirmation with Eddie, and he agreed that the baby's name would be Amazing Grace.

But why this name? I even wondered if she was going to be physically challenged, and that perhaps her name was chosen by God because she would be an overcomer. Once, during a visit with Pastor Valerie Holcomb, I told her the name of our baby. Pastor Valerie suggested we look up the word *amazing* in another language and use that translation for the first name, instead of just calling her "amazing." We took her suggestion and researched several foreign language books. Eddie and I both liked the Romanian translation for *amazing* — "amira." We chose the translation

Amira in lieu of calling her Amazing. Prior to Amira's birth, we never knew her gender; we just believed in our hearts she was a girl, or at least I did. Eddie was pretty flexible. However, with the God-given name of "Amazing Grace," he was hoping it was a girl.

In my seventh month of pregnancy, I prayed that God would heal me of the herpes because of the potential risk to our baby. Eddie agreed with me in prayer, as well, that God would heal me so that our little baby would not be at risk. In addition, we just wanted overall healing. Herpes is a very painful and uncomfortable venereal disease. The lesions produced by this disease can sometimes be unbearable. For a woman, it can be difficult to sit, stand, or walk comfortably during active stages. I can recall intense pain for up to three days before it would finally subside. I accepted this disease as a punishment for my past failures. In my own low opinion of myself, I felt that I needed some type of permanent reminder of what I had done in my past. The herpes was indeed permanent and incurable, and thus, my reminder. Yet, Eddie didn't deserve it. Though he never complained, my heart went out to him because he was exposed and at risk. And his heart and tender compassion went out to me as I suffered excruciating pain with each episode.

The Lord blessed Amira's delivery, keeping the herpes inactive. She was born naturally and with no complications. We were proud parents of a beautiful baby girl. Her older sister and brother were elated about the addition to our family.

At the writing of this book, it has been over ten years since Eddie and I prayed for God to heal me of herpes, and He did! We are not sure of the exact date of my healing, but we believe He healed me while I was pregnant with Amira. My last outbreak of herpes was in the seventh month of pregnancy when we both sought God for healing. Since that time, I have never had another herpes episode. I have had over ten glorious years of walking in the miraculous healing of the Lord.

Medical research concludes that herpes is an incurable disease. However, as the song goes, "Whose report will you believe? I will believe the report of the Lord! His Word says that I am healed!" Truly, God supernaturally healed me through the blood of Jesus. I never went through a prayer line; I never felt a rush of any kind go through my body. It was our mustard-seed faith and the gentle touch of God's healing power, grace, and mercy that healed me. I was miraculously healed from an incurable disease! To God be the glory forever and ever!

I believe that God especially honored my husband's commitment to love and cherish me unconditionally. In my spirit, I am convinced that because Eddie obeyed the voice of God, married me without wavering, and cherished me as if I were his virgin, he won favor with God. I am convinced that my husband's love for me so modeled God's love for the church that Eddie moved the heart of God, and God was merciful and healed my diseased body. And in keeping with His amazing grace, God also protected Eddie from the transference of the disease. God is so awesome! He really is all we ever need.

But there's one more facet to this story. Recently, I was talking to a man who speaks Arabic. He was taking down some information for me, and when I told him my daughter's name was Amira, He said to me, "Do you know what that means in Arabic?" Of course, I told him no. He told me that Amira in Arabic is translated as "princess." Needless to say, that really floored me. God's plan and purposes have been constantly unfolding in my life. As I look back, I can see that my daughter was named Amira not only because of God's amazing grace, but also because of His affirmation and His restoration of my life—He wanted to reaffirm to me through Amira that His view of me is truly as His princess.

God's Amazing Grace

How much does it cost; what is its price?
The value of it is more than one could pay.

Could it ever be purchased with the finest gold and silver?
Its cost would far exceed all the wealth this world could offer.

Can one invest in this great commodity?
The dividends come freely, without investment.

Then can one barter to acquire this great asset?
There is nothing to merit an equal exchange.

Surely, one must do something to be a benefactor!
One must do nothing; it cannot be earned.
Can the most upright be given careful consideration?
No, it is simply an unearned merit.

Are there strings attached? Loop holes perhaps?
It is simply freely given.
But how?
It is unmerited favor.
God's amazing grace cannot be earned.

We could never be good enough, right enough, or perfect enough
to deserve it.
His amazing grace saves, heals, and restores; it is everlasting.
God is Love.

God is Amazing and full of Grace.

Chapter Eleven

The Past Returns

When Amira was just two weeks old, Eddie and I returned to Christian House of Prayer so Pastor Holcomb could dedicate her to the Lord. Pastor Holcomb and Pastor Valerie invited us to their home for dinner after the service.

After dinner, Pastor Valerie invited me into another room because she wanted to talk with me privately. She told me she had heard something and wanted to know if it was true. She said that she was told I had had an affair with a certain pastor at another church. She immediately told me that she had come to my defense and had told the bearer of this news that I was Ms. City Princess and that they must have the wrong person. However, they had emphatically insisted that, no, I was the one.

The *shame* that I felt was unbelievable. I began to cry and cry. "Yes, it is true," I told her. At this point, it had been almost two years since it had happened, and I was crushed that it had come up again. I had been living with the scars and shame every day since it had happened. I had been silently dwelling within my own self-imposed prison of memories and the chains of my past. However, to hear that my past was being brought up again and to know that it was still confronting me was more than I felt I could bear.

Pastor Valerie remained Spirit-led throughout this entire disclosure. She was, of course, deeply saddened to hear that it was true, but she was also righteously indignant regarding the situation and how the Enemy had taken advantage of me. She encouraged me and prayed with me. I told her that I wanted it to be behind me, and that I had somehow, naively, perhaps, hoped that after nearly two years, it was. She asked if Eddie knew. "Yes," I said. "I told him before we were married. Eddie loves me so much. He said God had told him I was to be his wife. Therefore, Eddie married me in spite of my past." Pastor Valerie consoled me and loved me.

When I departed with Eddie that day, I told him about my conversation with Pastor Valerie. He was so hurt for me. He knew how challenged I had been in working through the issues of my past. I relayed to him how much love Pastor Valerie had showed me and that she hadn't judged me or scorned me. She had just held me and loved me, and that truly ministered to me.

The fact remained, however, that no matter what, my past was who I was. I knew that I couldn't run and I couldn't hide; but I could withdraw, and so I did. I would try to be low-keyed in the church and maintain a low profile. God had gifted me with writing skills for plays, skits, and poetry. I decided I would use them on occasion, but not too often, because I felt I didn't deserve to be used too much by God in the church. After all, I had failed Him. Consequently, I became my own judge and jury.

In the church in which I grew up, when people committed an "unpardonable transgression," they were barred from all activities, boards, and ministries, and had to sit in the front pew of the church as penance. They were under scrutiny and observation until released. I felt as if I, too, deserved similar treatment. Since I had no one to monitor my involvement, I monitored it myself. Sometimes, I would see myself really letting go and being used in my gifts of writing or in drama. But then I would abruptly pull back and examine what I was doing. "Who do you think you are?" I berated myself. If anyone knew, you wouldn't be doing anything. As a result, a cloud of shame, low self-worth, and heaviness constantly hovered over me. But I felt I deserved it. I became paranoid at the possibility of being in the presence of pastors and their wives unless I had developed a prior relationship with them before they had entered their God-ordained positions. To be in close proximity to any pastor and his wife was a constant reminder of my failure.

I have never met another minister like Pastor, nor has any other pastor ever approached me in an ungodly manner. In retrospect, I now know that, because I had never forgiven myself, I did not feel worthy to have a relationship with pastors and their wives, except on a very superficial level. Again, the Enemy was at work, sowing seeds of deception in my life; robbing me of my gifts, talents, and anointing; and ultimately postponing my destiny for as long as he could.

The Past Returns

Oh, no, could this be? Who still remembers when?
My past ever present, my sins lingering.
Tell me it's not so...how I want to vanish!
There is nowhere to run to, nowhere to hide.

I must accept that my past is who I am!
I have been a failure! Is there any hope?
Is it true that once doomed, always doomed?
Can His redemption help me to rise again?

I brought shame on my life; my name is ruined.
Can God redeem this wretched soul that I am?
Is it worth Your healing this broken vessel?
I am trying, Lord, to live a different life.

But the past, my failures, are ever present;
I feel so weak, so faint, and so ashamed.
Father God, I need You. Do You hear me now?
I know You are there, yet You seem so distant.

I weep before Your throne, I weep and I groan.
Your daughter feels the sorrow of all her past.
The accusing Enemy is all around.
He will give no peace to my troubled mind.

Will there be a day I rise in victory?
Father, Your daughter feels sorrow for her past.
I groan in agony, and shame covers me.
My pain is mine to bear; I am so burdened.

Lord, I want to offer all my pain to You,
But I'm too ashamed; I bear this pain alone.
The presence of darkness hovers over me.
Though I want to forget, my past is with me.

Chapter Twelve

The Unexpected

E ddie would listen to me when I would cry about my past. Of course, the biggest issue would always be Pastor. Eddie encouraged me to move forward, to give it to God once and for all. But I wrestled within myself because I felt it really wasn't God's problem. It wasn't God's fault that I carried all these weights. God had done enough for me, I reasoned. I would handle it—or so I thought.

One night, out of the clear blue, the pastor from the past called my house. Eddie answered the phone, and Pastor told him that his mother had died recently and he wanted to let me know, since I had known her. Eddie, though protective of me, did not perceive any underlying motives by this call; however, he remained cautious. He handed me the phone.

This was quite an awkward situation. It seemed too delicate to question Pastor's motives, given the circumstances. Because his mother had recently passed away, I decided to give my condolences and quickly say good-bye.

I thought it was strange that he would call me. It wasn't as if his mother and I had been very close, although I was sincerely sorry about her death. I guess he got our telephone number from information. Hearing from him when I had hoped never to hear from him again was disappointing—and upsetting.

Within two weeks, Pastor called again in the evening while we were all at home. Unfortunately, I answered the phone. This time, he called to cry about his mother's death. I felt very uncomfortable. It was obvious that he was upset and in despair about his mother. I listened and then told him that Eddie and I would pray for him.

When I got off the phone, I turned to Eddie and said, "I am not sure why Pastor is calling me." Eddie then assured me that he would talk to Pastor, should he ever call again.

A month or so later, I visited the Christian House of Prayer. I had gone there alone to meet with Pastor Valerie to discuss a business venture. She took me to lunch, and we had a productive meeting. Just as I was preparing to leave to return home, I told her that the pastor from my past had called me twice, and the reasons for his calls. She told me, in no uncertain terms, that the next time he called, if he called, I was to tell him never to call me again. She said that it didn't matter how sad he sounded. She expressed that it was a trick of the Enemy and that I had to be smarter than he was. I assured her that, if he called again, I would tell him. Pastor Valerie strongly reiterated that I must be the one to tell him not to call, since it was I whom Pastor sought.

Approximately a month later, Pastor did call. I was at home alone with Amira, and my other two children were in school. When I answered, he sounded as calm and collected as possible, as though it were just a routine call.

"Hello, Pat, and how are you?" he began. That is when I let him have it. I told him never to call my house again. I reiterated that I was a married woman, that I loved my husband, and that he had no right to call me. He explained that he was simply calling to say "Hi." I told him that I didn't want him to call to say "hi" or for any other reason. With authority, I boldly told him that I knew what he was trying to do, and I assured him that I wasn't interested! I angrily told him, "Don't ever call me again!" While he hesitated in saying good-bye, I hung up. After hanging up, I felt assured that there were no lingering doubts in his mind that I meant what I said. I had left him no room to wonder.

Though somewhat shaken by this occurrence, I felt that Pastor had finally gotten the message loud and clear. How dare the Enemy even think for a moment that he could destroy the new life God had given me! That evening, I told Eddie what had happened, and he was proud that I had shown boldness in standing up to this pastor.

Pastor never called my house again. However, one Sunday, Eddie and I went back to visit Pastors Nate and Valerie Holcomb at Christian House of Prayer. We, along with our guest from Covenant Church, where we were now attending, were invited to dinner after the service by Elder Hickson and his wife, Donna. When the church was smaller, Eddie and I would sometimes eat with Pastors Nate and Valerie when visiting. However, they were not able to join us this time. The church was growing at a phenomenal rate. They had already moved into their third church building, and they were still confessing, "People are standing in line to get in this church to hear the Word of God...." After the service, we all joined the Hicksons at a nearby restaurant for a delicious Sunday dinner.

Later, as we were finishing our meal, Donna, who has to be one of the wisest, most precious, Spirit-led women I have ever known, discreetly leaned over to me and said, "Pastor is right around the corner, near the door where you will exit." (Until that time, I was not aware that she knew of my affair with Pastor, but that day I was very glad she did.) She told me that his back was turned away from me, and that if I kept my back toward him as I walked out, he would probably never see me, even if he turned around. I appreciated the love with which this elder's wife covered me. The motivation of her heart was to protect me. I leaned over and told Eddie.

As we departed, I was able to leave unnoticed and unseen by Pastor. It was hard to believe that we were both in the same restaurant. It had been almost two years since I had been back to visit this church and this city. Who would believe that this pastor from my past would be in the same restaurant at the same time that I was? The Enemy had a plan, but it was thwarted. I was glad Donna was informed about my past. I thanked her for looking out for me. She could have questioned me for details. After all, she had just saved me from a very humiliating, embarrassing moment—perhaps I did owe her some explanation regarding my past. But she never questioned me. She did what God told her to do, and that was it. She could have looked down on me, but instead, she loved me and continued to visit with me as though this had never happened. I will never forget her kindness and her protective love.

The Unexpected
Dedicated to the "Elder's Wife"

We ate Sunday dinner, and laughed and talked.
Who would ever have imagined the thought
That in the restaurant this pastor would be
Right there in our presence, for us to see?

I enjoyed all the topics we discussed,
Then our conversation was quickly hushed.
You told me that he, too, was dining there,
And close by—he was dangerously near.

You told us how we could quietly leave
And never by him be perceived.
And with this plan we prepared to go,
To leave at once, so he would never know,
Never have a reason for stopping by,
And never even attempt to try.

Very carefully we stood up to go;
We passed by his table; he did not know
That you had just led us swiftly away.
That you'd heard the voice of God and obeyed.

Your heart was pure, and your motives divine,
Your love was so real; your words were so kind.
You kept me from facing even more shame
By having to see this pastor again.

I thank you, dear sister, for being there.
I am so glad that you were made aware,
And of His grace were a true reflection,
A vessel for God's loving protection.

Chapter Thirteen

The Presence of Evil

E ddie and I were now in our fifth year of marriage. I was
still in college. Eddie had insisted that I finish my educa-
tion; he said he wanted me to have my bachelor's degree
because he knew how much it meant to me. Eddie loved and
cared for me in a way that was God-inspired. He protected me
and watched over me like an eagle.

Though my husband is an easygoing person, there is an inner
fire within him that, when empowered by the Holy Spirit, can be
transformed into the aggressiveness of a fighting warrior. As you
read about this part of my life, you will discover the significance
of why God gave me a husband with such a mighty warring
spirit.

As I unfold this chapter, I request that you be open and ask
God to illuminate your understanding. Ask God to give you
revelatory insight into the reality of spiritual warfare so that you
may benefit by what I am about to share. Know this, the Enemy is
out to torment God's people because we are a threat to Satan's
kingdom. May God enable you to grasp the importance of knowing the defense that we have against principalities and powers in
high places (Ephesians 6:12).

It is my prayer that, once you read this, you will be compelled
to guard your purity and your relationship with God. Although I
was a born-again Christian, I was still open to the attacks of the
Enemy and did not have a biblical understanding of how to close
the door to them. I didn't realize that certain parts of my soul still
needed to be delivered from the soul-ties that I talked about in
chapter 4. I was still being attacked by the Enemy because there

were certain open doors in my life that allowed him to do so, including unforgiveness.

Open doors to demonic activity can come about through various avenues. It is important to know how the Devil has gained access to our lives. We should ask ourselves, "How was the door opened?" Once we know the answer to this, we will discover how to close the door. Gaining victory in the very area where the door was opened is the key to making sure that the door closes and remains closed.

There are five ways the Enemy gains access to our lives. I will briefly mention them and then discuss two of these ways, soul-ties and unforgiveness, and how they affected my life.

The four main ways in which the Enemy gains a legal right to our lives through open doors are

1. Bloodline or generational curses (Exodus 20:5)
2. Personal sin (Psalm 66:18; Ephesians 4:26–27)
3. Soul-ties (1 Corinthians 6:15–16)
4. Unforgiveness (Matthew 6:14–15)

The Enemy may also try to gain an illegal entrance into our lives. For this reason, I will include a fifth category.

5. The Trespasser (1 Peter 5:8). This open door occurs when someone is caught at a time of weakness caused by trauma, disappointment, lust, greed, selfishness, and other things that our flesh readily embraces when it is weak.

Because I had allowed some of these open doors in my life, I became weighed down with the presence of evil spirits. As you know, in my first marriage, my husband and I had both been involved in extramarital affairs. There had also been my affair with the pastor, who had been bisexual in his past. My relationship with him had exposed me to a connection with all his former bed partners. The accumulation of my sordid sexual past had left me with these unsevered soul-ties, as well as "open doors" for the presence of evil spirits in my life. As a matter of fact, nights were restless and fearful for me. I felt tortured at night by an evil presence, which I could feel and sense. It was horrible.

Soul-ties are generally developed between two human beings through ungodly sexual or emotional attachments, but they can also occur in the spiritual realm with an evil embodiment. I was to discover that the demon sent to torment me was what is known as an incubus spirit—a sexual demon. Satan's desire is to destroy the church through whatever means he can. An incubus desires to gain a stronghold so that he can control you in the realm of your fleshly desires. For the purposes of this book, I'll call the domain of our fleshly desires the "soulish" realm. Satan also desires to have control over your descendants, as well.

The calling card of an incubus is often pornography. As you know, indulgence in pornography takes place in the soulish realm. This area can be, and is, a stronghold for many. A stronghold is indeed a control factor in one's life. An incubus desires to control your body, soul, and mind (or spirit)—the three-part being of man. (See 1 Thessalonians 5:23.) It is very influential. Its presence can come about because of our ancestral backgrounds, as well as through direct soul-ties. Often, when coming through the bloodline, this spirit can be latent for a number of years. However, once sexual impurity occurs, it can open the gateway for an incubus spirit to gain access to one's life.

To overcome an evil presence, you need to be delivered and to come under the blood of Jesus. Then, you must learn to stay in that state of freedom. The Enemy will always try to gain access to your life, but staying in the Word and wearing the full armor of God is the key to your success and power over Satan. Even though the Devil tried to tempt Jesus, He was the only person who could say that Satan had no place in Him (John 14:30). All of us, however, are vulnerable to Satan's attacks when there are open doors in our lives. There are places in all of us where the Enemy can come back and try to touch us.

The believer's deliverance can be obtained and sustained by the power of God's Word as all doors are closed to Satan. Without an open door, he can't get in. He may be on the sidelines trying to intimidate, but he can't get in to touch us if he has no access.

The evil spirit who tormented me manifested itself in silhouette form and appeared to be about eight feet tall. It would walk into my bedroom as Eddie and I slept. I would awaken, and my body would go into a trancelike state, as if frozen and unable to move. Sometimes, before entering my room, this demon would be preceded by little demonic imps with high-pitched voices. They stood about eight inches off the ground. My body could not move at all. I could only cry out in my mind, "Jesus!" It was obvious they could hear my thoughts because I would get a reaction from them; these little imps would cower at the mighty name of Jesus, but after cowering, they would continue with their antagonizing ways until repeated calls on the name of Jesus would cause them to flee.

This eight-foot demon was an incubus, a sexual demon from the pit of hell. I remember closing my eyes as he came and stood by my bed the first time. Few people understand demons, but they are on a mission. They have a plan for you if you submit, and a plan for you if you resist. They are sent to rule you, govern you, and control you. However, in the midst of their control, God can still be reached. The Lord heard my cry when I uttered "Jesus" in the spirit-realm. When the incubus heard "Jesus," it had no choice but to submit to the power that is in that name. When I initially called upon the name of Jesus, the incubus showed strong resistance by trying to choke me, smash my body against the bed, and torment me with fear. I called again on the name of Jesus, and this time he fled. Though this spirit had a powerful presence, it was too weak to withstand the power in the name of Jesus.

What an awful, fearful, confusing experience that was. It was the first time I had encountered such a presence. It was very foreign to me, yet I knew it was demonic. Initially, I was too ashamed to tell my husband that a sex demon was coming into the room at night. I knew I had not invited this grotesque creature, but how could I explain its evil presence to my husband? After I experienced the third attack, I knew that this incubus spirit was planning on making regular visits. Though it would flee when I called on the name of Jesus, it still kept coming back! I needed Eddie to protect me from it. I told my husband, and he listened intently. Eddie was uncertain about it and felt he needed more instruction regarding the spiritual realm and how to conduct spiritual warfare. He had always tried to protect me and help me, but this time he needed more spiritual guidance. Until he obtained direction, Eddie did all he knew to do—pray.

We were both aware that this battle was not against "flesh and blood" but an evil spiritual power (Ephesians 6:12). It could be fought only in the spirit-realm with the necessary weapons given by God. Eddie and I sought God for insight regarding how to effectively approach this demon who was desperately trying to control my life with fear.

Somehow, we had heard of an elder in our church named Jessye Ruffin. We were told that she was involved in deliverance ministry and spiritual warfare, and had great insight in this area. However, because I was ashamed, I had planned to withhold some of the details when I met with Jessye. We made an appointment, and I told her, as discreetly as possible, what was happening to me. She knew exactly what this demon was and what he had been sent to do. I didn't have to give her any details; she discerned its roots by the Spirit.

Jessye told me the demon was an incubus. Although throughout this chapter I have referred to this demon as an incubus, I was totally unaware of its roots and its origin at the time that I was first experiencing the encounters. I told her that I was very afraid of it. She told me to pray that God would reveal its name to us so that we could directly call it out and address it in the spirit-realm. Jessye also explained that this demon had come as a result of an open door caused by sexual impurity in my life. She told Eddie and me that we needed to break the soul-ties. This was the first time Eddie and I had ever heard of soul-ties. She instructed Eddie how to pray over me, and told me that if I felt more comfortable with the light on at night, to keep it on. She gave us Scriptures to pray and told Eddie that he was my spiritual covering and he had authority through Christ to rebuke those evil spirits on my behalf. Then she and her husband, Jerry, covered us in prayer. (It has been over ten years since our initial meeting with Pastor Jessye. Today, she and her husband are the Associate Pastors of the healing and deliverance ministry at Covenant Church.) God used Pastor Jessye to pave the road for my eventual escape from the spiritual darkness that had encompassed me.

During this same time frame, Pastor Mike Hayes, our pastor, requested our church to join him in a Daniel's Fast. This type of fast is conducted according to Daniel 10:2–3. (As you read further on in this Scripture passage, you will see that Daniel's prayer was answered in Daniel 10:12.) For those of us at Covenant who were seeking answers to questions and concerns in our lives and wanted to hear from God, the Daniel's Fast was timely. I, along with many members in the church, went on the twenty-one day fast. Eddie had decided that he would go on a forty-day liquid fast consecration and refrain from all solid foods. My husband stands six feet tall; he has broad shoulders and a slim physique. During this forty-day liquid fast, Eddie lost twenty-two pounds. His body was very lean, but his Spirit was a giant waiting for a battle to happen. The power and anointing that Eddie possessed was by the authority of the Holy Spirit.

One night, in our bedroom, as I shared my fears concerning this evil presence that still kept tormenting me, my husband felt inspired to aggressively pray for me. There was a fresh power and anointing resident in Eddie. He laid hands on me and began to wage war in the Spirit for my freedom.

Eddie spent several hours in prayer and warfare, and after about three hours, the evil presence that had seemed so over-bearing was completely gone. I could feel its departure. Though I was a born-again believer and God was Lord over my life, I real-ized that a part of my soul had still been controlled by Satan. He had been given legal rights to torment me because of the open doors in my life that needed to be closed. I believe that all the soul-ties I had ever possessed were broken off me as God used Eddie to fight in the Spirit for my sake. Thank God for my hus-band! God worked through him to bring deliverance to my soul, and I experienced the classic signs of release: my spirit was made whole, and I no longer felt fragmented. There was such an awe-some presence of peace upon me as I lay down to sleep that night. I slept many, many peaceful nights thereafter.

As long as I live, I will never forget the experience I had with this demon and his tormenting imps. The memory of this experi-ence makes me want to demolish Satan's kingdom with powerful and unrelenting spiritual warfare.

My situation with the incubus spirit was not an isolated inci-dent. It is more common than people think; it is just that those who are attacked do not discuss it for fear that people will think they are crazy or evil because they are exposed to such an evil force. I have shared my experience because I want others to feel the liberty to come forth and seek prayer for their deliverance. The fierceness of this type of spirit is real, and it is horrid. I know there are other women who need to be set free from it.

In the ladies' conferences at which I have been invited as a guest speaker, I have met women who have secretly expressed to me that they, too, have encountered the incubus spirit. They state that they were not aware that it had a name and that there were others beside themselves who have undergone such horrendous experiences.

At one of the conferences, there was a woman who came up to me with tears in her eyes. She thanked me for sharing my testimony, saying that she also had been plagued with this evil spirit. She stated that it would torment her at night in unbelievable ways. She also said that she had felt isolated in her torment and had never realized there were others who were being tortured by this demon. As a result, this dear woman had kept her demonic attacks a secret, and no one had ever prayed for her concerning them. She said she thought that there was nothing she could do about it because this demon would never leave her alone. She was also afraid no one could understand if she tried to explain what was happening.

Unfortunately, when this woman came up to talk to me, there were other women all around me, and I could not adequately minister to her as I desired. But I told her that I would be praying for her release. As she told me that she would buy my book, her eyes were desperate, and my heart went out to her.

The next morning, at the end of the final meeting of the conference, this woman eagerly ran up to me. She hugged me and told me she was free. She said she had completed my book when she returned to her hotel room, and then she had told one of the female leaders from her church about the attacks. This leader and two other ladies prayed for her for several hours, until she said she was certain that she was free. She told me, "I know that it is gone." She hugged me again and thanked me for sharing my testimony, telling me, "I will never forget you."

Only God could have brought such peace to this woman who only the day before had been desperately reaching out for hope and for a chance to experience freedom from this demon.

I would now like to talk to you about a second way the Enemy gained access to my life to afflict me because I feel it's important to let you know that unforgiveness toward yourself or others will give Satan legal access to your life. Even though I had been delivered from the incubus spirit, I still experienced subtle demonic attacks from Satan throughout my years of shame. It wasn't until I totally forgave myself and allowed God to completely restore me that I had dominion over the powers of darkness. They no longer have legal access to my life.

Without an access key, Satan cannot get in. Remember that unforgiveness and sexual sins are two of the keys that give Satan legal access to your life to bring torment. It is also important to note that Satan has different plans for different people. He specifically targets the people of God that He fears will be used to destroy His evil works. If Satan is haunting you about your failures and is constantly tormenting you, then know this: God has great plans for your future! All you have to do is put Satan in his place by putting him out of your life.

Based upon my experience with the powers of darkness, I have no fear, because I have learned that Satan's greatest enemy is one who is armed in the power of the Word. Satan knows I am armed and dangerous. I am lethal where He is concerned.

Although God had restored me, given me Eddie, and blessed me in many ways, I continued to be the judge and jury of my soul as the years passed. Unforgiveness is something through which the Enemy tries to conceal our true feelings. We are taught that, as Christians, we should forgive. Therefore, we have almost rehearsed our response to forgiveness. We simply say with our lips, "I forgive you," as if by saying it, it becomes reality. In fact, saying it can make us feel as if we have accomplished the act of forgiving, but in essence, we still struggle with the heart issues surrounding the cause of the unforgiveness. Being able to say "I forgive you" is not what makes the true act of forgiveness occur. Forgiveness comes about through a change of heart. Forgiveness means that when the cause or the subject matter of your unforgiveness arises, you do not relive it, become emotionally entangled by it, or desire vengeance against the offending party.

In my situation, I found it hard to tell myself that I truly forgave myself—that I forgave Patricia for her failures with the pastor. Every time the subject matter or the thought of my offense would come to the forefront of my mind, I would relive it, become emotionally entangled with it, and take vengeance against myself by holding myself captive to my painful memories.

I was holding myself in debt to my failure in Christ. I felt I had a right to hold myself captive. But, in fact, I had to cancel the debt in order to be set free. In other words, I had to release myself from the bondage of a debt that I could not pay. The truth that Jesus' blood paid the price for all of my debts had to become a living reality to me in order for me to let go of my past and allow my debts to be cancelled.

Superficial forgiveness is babble. True forgiveness comes from the heart. It is the grace of God that floods you with His love to make the process of forgiveness a reality. When we forgive, we must become angry at the real perpetrator. We must learn to hate the real enemy, the Devil, and see the people he manipulates against us as victims of his plans, in the same way we have been manipulated as his victims. Self-forgiveness works in a similar way. You must realize that Satan is using you against yourself. Being able to walk in true forgiveness is powerful. It is so powerful that it can disengage demonic access to your life and close the door to demonic activity.

Had it not been for the grace of God in my own life, I don't know what I would have done. God kept me covered through the name of Jesus, and He will do the same for you.

The name of the LORD is a strong tower; the righteous run to it and are safe. (Proverbs 18:10)

We are troubled on every side, yet not distressed; we are perplexed, but not in despair; persecuted, but not forsaken; cast down, but not destroyed. (2 Corinthians 4:8–9 KJV)

The Lord God reigns!

The Presence of Evil

I gave away the purity of my soul
In exchange for a web of soul-ties
That entangled my very being,
Until I became a fraction of who I was.

I chose the path of folly,
And indulged in forbidden pleasures.
Unknowingly, I opened a door
That only deliverance could shut.

And through this open door
Satan and his troops came marching in.
They tormented, shamed, and mocked me,
And I hung my head in fear and despair.

I did not know what had happened
To bring about this fierce attack.
Where had these tormentors come from?
Who was responsible for their presence?

Then I learned that I had opened the door.
I had invited them into my life!
They had legal access to torment me.
These demons desired my very soul!

But then I learned how to war in the Spirit,
How to put on the armor of God's Word.
The priest of my home prepared for the battle,
Defending me through the blood of the Lamb.

Through the power in Jesus' name,
They had to flee, and soon obeyed.
The door was shut, the way was blocked,
The presence of evil had to flee!

And Jesus became the Lifter of my head.

Chapter Fourteen

The Letter

After seven years of membership at Covenant Church, I decided to mail a letter of disclosure to my pastors, Mike and Kathy Hayes. I did not ask for a response from them. In fact, I didn't want one. My letter was a letter of confession. I openly acknowledged to them my illicit relationship with this pastor from my past. I felt I had to tell them. It had become such a weight on my shoulders. I told myself that it was about time they knew "who I really was." This shameful incident was always before me, and I could not get it off my mind. There was so much guilt and heaviness associated with this painful memory. I wanted all the flashbacks to just go away, but they lingered, day after day, night after night.

Even though I had been delivered from the torment of the incubus spirit, my memory of the past was as vivid as if it had happened yesterday. It was as if I were reliving it all over again. I began to wrestle more and more with the shame of my past. I became very disappointed in myself and started feeling a sense of incompetence, unworthiness, and inadequacy. I thought that if I could just inform my pastors about my past, then maybe this dark, heavy cloud would be lifted, and I would be free of the shame. So I mailed them a brief letter as an act of open confession.

Not the least bit daunted, Pastors Mike and Kathy continued to love me in the same way. They treated me as if they had never been made aware of my past. I was blessed by their love for me, for I knew it was genuine. I never chose to personally approach them to discuss the issue, because I didn't really want to. All I really wanted was to shed the weight of my hidden past. I wanted to break the invisible chains that held me captive. How I wanted to be free — and writing that letter of confession to my pastors was a step in the right direction. However, despite this bold admission of my past guilt, I continued to silently hold onto my veil of shame, because, inwardly, I still would not forgive myself. You can take all the "right steps" to freedom, but if you do not forgive yourself, then you have not accomplished anything by taking those right steps. It's either all or nothing. Your motives may be good, but only Jesus can give you the grace to release it all to Him.

Despite the fact that Covenant Church has a growing and thriving ministry, and that Pastor Mike is dynamically anointed to teach the Word, I would not allow myself to be set free. I seemed to have a personal vendetta against myself, forbidding the release of my heavy burden.

In my years as a believer, I had always been challenged with reading my Bible consistently. Every time I attempted to study the Bible, there always seemed to be a block to my understanding of it, as well as my enthusiasm for reading it. However, I longed to love God's Word. I had heard others share about their growth through reading the Bible, but for me, it was an arduous under-taking. The little Scripture I did consume kept me at a notch above the Enemy's strategy to destroy me. I am thankful I consumed what I did. Since I was lacking the power in my life that comes through God's Word, I consistently struggled with shame; I would not allow God's Word to cleanse me from my inability to forgive myself. If it had not been for the grace of God, I easily could have transitioned into a depressed state of mind. Satan con-tinually told me the same message over and over again: "If they only knew, what would they think of you?" Though the Enemy tried to destroy me with his accusations, the Holy Spirit was ever present to endow me with His mercy.

Chapter Fifteen

Secrets of the Heart

While yet in my seventh year at Covenant Church, I attempted another breakthrough from my ever present world of shame. As an amateur playwright, I would often write plays for various groups within the church or for special events (for example, children's ministry, youth, singles, and Black History Month). At that time, I decided to write a play for the singles ministry. It would be about a young woman who was continually making wrong choices for the sake of love, but who finally would learn to make the right decision in the end. It would be a play about me. I knew no one would ever guess that this play was indirectly telling my story, and it would serve as a way for me to write the conclusion to a journey that had not yet come to an end for me, even after seven years. I called the play *The Perfect Gentleman* and wrote an ending for it that I so yearned for in my own life.

I held auditions for the play, and several cast members were selected. The lady whom I chose to play my part was perfect. As an actress, she was able to accurately portray the weight that I carried in real life. She expressed the pain of my soul through her acting, which existed with me every day. She could feel it and understand it. This actress, Constance Sollien, was the heartbeat of the play.

In the story, her character, Casey, has just met a man named Grant whom she thinks she adores. Grant represents the pastor. He tells her all the things she wants to hear, and Casey is on cloud nine. Grant assures her that she is everything, and Casey believes him. But Grant has greater plans for her, plans to lure her into a deep relationship that will entangle her soul.

One night, after coming home from a date with Grant, Casey's roommate, Anita, waits up for her to share with her about the perfect gentleman she has met. Anita is as bubbly as Casey, and they both want to talk about their love lives. Casey goes on and on about Grant. Finally, Anita is able to share about her newfound love. As the conversation develops, Anita discloses that her new love is Jesus, and that He is a perfect gentleman. She talks of how she danced before Him and with Him, and how He embraced her with His love. She explains that there is no sorrow or rejection with Him. As Casey listens, she finds it hard to understand having such a relationship with someone you can't see or touch. Anita tries hard to convince her of how real Jesus is and how He has forgiven her, yet Casey can't comprehend it. She tells Anita that her sins could never be washed away because she has so many stains in her life. Anita tells her that Jesus can make her clean. She even tells Casey that there really are godly men who go to church, who respect women, and who won't ask them to have sex before marriage. Casey is incredulous and begins to laugh. She concludes that these men must be the "rejects" of society, "the ones nobody wants." Her response is, "These are duds, aren't they?"

But after she falls asleep that night, she begins to dream about her conversation with Anita, and in her dream, she has on a dress spotted with stains. She finds herself in a church, a church filled with men engaged in a Bible study. As she stands in the corner of this church, she observes the men praying as they conclude their study. She quickly goes over to them and begins to introduce herself as she looks them up and down. She blurts out to them that she has heard about them and their kind from her friend Anita. The men are very confused, and Casey carries the conversation in another direction. She finally can't stand it, and she asks them if they are pure to the point of not having sex. The men respond with character; they tell her they don't focus on that, and they believe in waiting until they are married.

The conversation continues until one of the men tells Casey that God has brought her to their church. They tell her that she is in the right place at the right time. They offer to show her the way, but she tells them that she cannot go down the path they are on because she is so stained, and that she is too ashamed to meet this Perfect Gentleman Anita has told her about. The godly men tell her that He is waiting to meet her. But Casey turns away, saying that she's not ready, not now. She tells them that her stains are permanent, and she asks them if they have ever had a stain that, no matter how much you wash it, never comes out. She assures them that this is her predicament. Yet when she hears that Jesus sees the beauty in her, she says she wants to meet Him. She asks the men to tell Jesus that she has never met a perfect gentleman before, and then she asks them to show her the way to Him.

As she prepares to meet Him, in comes a well-dressed man, with a top hat, a cane, and a black and white suit. There is alluring music, and his eyes meet hers. It is Grant. He comes up to her and tells her that he is the gentleman who has been waiting for her. "I've been waiting for you....Let's spend time together. I'm your perfect gentleman." Casey is surprised. She looks back at the godly men, and then she asks, "You're the perfect gentleman? You're different from what I thought." And then she tells him that he looks familiar, like someone she has met before. Grant tells her that he knows what she needs and what she wants, and he lures her to dance with him. She is taken in by his words, his looks, and his passion for her. She gets caught up in the moment and forgets all about her stains and about meeting Jesus. Grant tells her, "We'll dance all night, and I will embrace you with my love. You belong to *me*." Casey is thrilled. She feels that at last she has found the one; he has finally arrived.

The godly men try to reach her; they tell her that he is not the one and that he is deceiving her. Grant pushes them away as he continues to dance with Casey, spinning her around and making her focus on him. Grant turns to the men and tells them, "You heard her. She has been waiting for me all her life. She is mine." Then he looks at Casey and tells her to leave with him.

He begins to forcefully pull on her, and suddenly Casey realizes that he does not have gentlemanlike traits. At this point, the godly men once again tell her that the Perfect Gentleman is waiting for her. Grant tells her, "No." He tries to reach for her, and tells her that this is her last chance, to "Come at once!"

Casey realizes that she almost made another bad decision. She turns away from Grant and asks the godly men to show her the way. Grant tries to reach for her, and the men turn to him with great power as they motion for him to leave. Grant quickly cowers and leaves the premises without another word.

The music in the room changes, and it is peaceful and calm. The godly men beckon to Casey to go in the direction of an altar that is straight ahead of her. She walks toward this altar and kneels in Jesus' presence. There she finds the love, the peace, the Perfect Gentleman. She feels His embrace as she weeps. She says, "I come just as I am, Lord. Wash me and make me clean. Show me the way." The spotted garment that she was wearing comes off, revealing a clean garment underneath, and she realizes that, for the first time, she is a woman without stains. She begins to dance before the Lord, and she exclaims that she feels as though she has wings. Happily, she says, "I have finally found my Perfect Gentleman," and the dream ends.

The next morning, Casey awakes, and she verbally accepts the Lord into her life. She runs to tell Anita, who embraces her and rejoices with her. Casey vows to keep herself pure before God, and she does. She trusts Him to send her a true man of God for her husband.

As I wrote this play, I wept. And I wept at every production. The play was performed at Covenant Church and two other churches as an outreach. Oh, how I wanted to be like Casey, to dance freely before Him. Though I had been walking in purity since I met my husband, I was not yet walking in freedom, like Casey.

One night after a production, I talked with Constance, the young lady who was cast as Casey. In an attempt to get free, perhaps to bring closure to my pain, I told her that she was actually playing the part of me in the play. She looked at me and said, "Actually, Patricia, I am playing the part of me. My life in the past has been so similar to Casey's." Then, in a few words, with my head hanging down, I told her that I had fallen with a pastor. She looked at me and, with carefully chosen words and a gentle touch to my hand, said, "He was a man, not your pastor, Patricia." As she said those words, a tear rolled down my face. I said to her, "Promise me you will never tell anyone," and she agreed.

As I lay in bed that night, I didn't feel much relief from having told her about my shameful secret. As a matter of fact, I wished I hadn't. I had been vulnerable at a time of emotional weakness, and I had shared my deep, deep secret. I was mad at myself. All I could do was hope she would never tell anyone. I didn't think she would, but I was mad at myself for having told her. Although I had known Constance for several years, and I knew she was trustworthy and a precious woman of God, I still felt awkward about having shared my past with her. I was supposed to have kept it a secret, and I had blown it. Eddie felt it was a good thing to disclose it, but I told him that I wished I hadn't. I told him that I was not going to share it with anyone else.

Constance and I talked again, and once more, I requested that she keep it a secret, and she promised she would. I felt much better, but I was still mad at myself for being vulnerable. "I have to be stronger. I can't go around telling people just because I get emotional," I thought to myself.

Even though writing and directing *The Perfect Gentleman* helped to minister to the secrets of my heart, and some fallow ground had been plowed in my spirit, I once again hardened and opted to handle my shame myself.

Chapter Sixteen

Tension in the Camp

Time continued to pass, and I graduated from college. Soon afterward, I started a private practice as a vocational rehabilitation counselor. I provided services to injured workers under a federal program, as well as to physically and mentally disabled clients. As my career progressed, I extended my services to the court system as a vocational expert. My degree was very versatile, and I was given numerous opportunities to use it as an entrepreneur. My career had become a reality because my husband believed in me and supported me. As God blessed me with the best contracts and allowed me to excel, my college degree and achievements became my self-worth, and my career became my source of identity. I had now acquired tangible proof that I was not a total failure. I felt significant as I hid in the busyness of my growing career.

However, as time progressed, my baggage of shame became heavier and heavier. It became increasingly difficult for me to forgive myself. Unfortunately, I became angry toward men as a result of my unforgiveness. Sometimes I would take my anger out on Eddie and would overlook the fact that he was not the one who had hurt me. Yet, I rationalized, he belonged to their "tribe." He was a man like all the others.

Then, as if we were hit by a bolt of lightening, Eddie and I began to experience challenges in our marriage. The Enemy was definitely at work. Satan used my harbored anger toward men as a device to bring dissension between Eddie and me. I was unaware that my final hour of redemption was drawing near. I just knew that Satan was trying whatever he could to put tension between us.

The Enemy started pulling tricks from every corner. Eddie and I experienced several months of tension in our marriage as we struggled to compromise and deal with the escalating conflict. It was heartbreaking to see the strong resistance we had toward one other, which was creating a severe marital imbalance. The Enemy was deceiving us both; it wasn't until the blinders were removed from our eyes that we could see the craftiness of Satan. He was out to destroy the most precious relationship I had ever experienced and known with a man. Our marriage is a gift from God, and Satan's plan was to bring division so he could interfere with the plan of God for our lives. However, peace entered our relationship as we submitted our wills to the headship of Jesus. We sought counsel from our elders, Wayne and Jill Blue. They prayed for us, covered us, and stood with us for God's complete restoration of our marriage. Within a short period of time, our relationship began to blossom, and the Holy Spirit knitted our hearts together again as Eddie and I submitted our marriage to God.

'Til Death Do Us Part

In sickness and health, for richer, for poorer.
No matter the trials, our love would endure.
We both were committed 'til death do us part.
Those were the words that we spoke from our heart.

Steadfast and solid with every wind that blew,
Our love was undying, would always be true.
We held onto the vows that we had decreed.
Nothing could alter what we had agreed.

Then came the day our vows were sorely tested,
Along with the prayers that we had invested.
At first we wavered in our desire to fight.
We tried to do everything we thought was right.

Vain Ahab and Jezebel stood in our place;
This was the biggest test we would ever face.
The knight and his princess had now been deceived.
Our spirits within were increasingly grieved.

We had turned our hearts from what we knew was true,
And forgotten the vows when we'd said, "I do."
Together we stand, but divided we fall.
We had lost the vision, our oneness, our call.

We humbled our spirits and turned to the Lord.
Together we knelt and put away the sword.
God hearkened to us, and He answered our prayer.
And faithfully freed us from the wicked snare.

Both of us had a real change of mind and heart.
We renewed our covenant — 'Til death do us part.
The scales then fell from our blinded eyes.
God was again the true center of our lives.

Chapter Seventeen

My Alabaster Box

A s I approached my eleventh year of marriage to Eddie, it became obvious that I was stooped in spirit. I had been carrying the same baggage for nearly twelve years. The weight was almost unbearable. Somehow, I had managed the weight by shifting it and rearranging it, but never had I conceived I'd ever dismantle it.

I began talking to the Lord about it. I told Him I was tired and weary. My journey had been a long and tedious one, with so little joy along the way. I wanted to feel the living waters flowing through me, as I had when I first accepted Jesus as my Lord and Savior. I wanted to feel free and to dance before His presence with joy. I told the Lord that I was ready to release it to Him. I didn't quite know how to let this awesome burden go. It had been such an intricate part of my life.

I thought about Pastor Mike and Pastor Kathy, and how they often ministered to our church body regarding the joy and release that comes through a transparent lifestyle. (God had also used them, as well as Pastors Nate and Valerie Holcomb, to restore my faith in pastoral leadership once again.) I began to meditate more and more on becoming transparent. The victory of becoming an overcomer after all these years was a desire that began to grow in me. Although I was still constantly reminded of my failure, its impact was losing its power to my increasing desire for freedom.

I shared with Eddie my desire to be free. He told me that he was in agreement, for he, too, wanted me to be released. Finally, I decided I would open my "alabaster box." There is an account in the New Testament of a woman, described as a "sinner," who came to Jesus carrying an alabaster box, or flask. In it was a very costly, fragrant oil, and she anointed Jesus with it. It is a picture of her offering everything she had and everything she was to Jesus. Jesus told her that her sins were forgiven, and He restored her to God.

I was familiar with the weighty contents of my own alabaster box all too well. It consisted of pain, unforgiveness, anger, failure, impurity, low self-esteem, fear, grief, and shame. My alabaster box was full and heavy. I wanted to bring it to Jesus. I wanted to empty its contents, to exchange them for something good. "I am ready to be healed," I told the Lord. "I want to be completely healed." Shortly after saying this sincere prayer, things began to change in my life. I still had my alabaster box, but I could sense it would soon be emptied of its contents. My mind was being renewed as I slowly began to latch on to God's promises for me. God's promises are sure and amen (2 Corinthians 1:20).

For I know the thoughts and plans that I have for you, says the Lord, thoughts and plans for welfare and peace and not for evil, to give you hope in your final outcome. (Jeremiah 29:11 AMP)

One day, as my elder, Jill Blue, and I were returning home from visiting one of our church members who was in the hospital, I decided to tell her about my past. To share my hidden twelve-year secret was a courageous step for me, even though I had previously shared it with Constance, the woman who had taken my role in the play. Yet, more than that, I felt that to do so was to begin the process of opening my alabaster box. As she was talking, I was trying to determine the approach I would take in disclosing my story. At first, we talked about many topics in general. Then, without delay, I told her I would like to share something with her. Jill responded, "Sure." I paused for a moment. I knew this was it; I had no plans to change my mind; I was going to tell her my secret no matter what. I had Jill's undivided attention as she sat there waiting for me to begin. And so I did. I told her the story from the beginning to the end. As a matter of fact, before we knew it, we were parked in front of my house.

Jill was the first person I told my story to with liberty and with a strong desire for freedom as I shared it with her. Jill's response was so gentle and so reassuring. Her words confirmed that my character over the years had been such that I could not be compared to the woman in the story that she was hearing. "Patricia, it's like you are telling me about someone else, not you; there is nothing about you that would ever make me think that," she said softly. Her words of affirmation comforted me as she remarked that I now walked in a manner diametrically opposed to where I had once been. Jill continued to listen, offer support, and give comforting words as I became more emotional and started to cry.

As I concluded our conversation, I told her that I was thinking about writing a book to help others who might be familiar with the same type of shame and bondage, for I myself knew of no one who could relate personally to this difficult journey. There had been no one from within the church who could give me a success story about how they came out of such a degrading situation. During my darkest hours, I had so needed to hear how someone else had made it through my own type of ordeal and agony. Yet, I had never heard a testimony, seen a book, or even read an article that addressed the issue of shame and the battle of overcoming such an incident.

I gave Jill a quick hug. She thanked me for sharing my story and agreed that should I write a book, for it would bless those who needed answers and consolation. Jill also commended the husband that God had given me. "Yes, Eddie is my gift from God," I told her.

What a contrast this experience was to the time I had disclosed my past to Constance. Although she had responded with compassion and acceptance, at that point I was still under my strict, self-imposed regime, and I had experienced remorse and regret instead of freedom after having shared it. In the first instance, I was still being held captive as I attempted to disclose the secrets of my heart, but this time, I was truly entering into freedom—there was no condemnation hanging on me.

As I got out of Jill's car and approached my front door, I felt such a sense of victory and freedom. I had done it! I had disclosed my darkest secret. At this point, my alabaster box lay open. I peered inside. Fear was no longer there.

Section Three:
Hope and a Future

Chapter Eighteen

Saturated with His Word

In the midst of my determination to speak out about my past, contemporary gospel artist Vicki Yohé came to our church. An anointed, gifted woman of God, her music ministered to me in a special way. God began to use her music to bring healing and strength to my spirit. I purchased two of her tapes that had the songs that ministered to me most, and I played "Hold Me like a Baby" and "The Mercy Seat" over and over again. I would play "The Mercy Seat" while I was at home alone during the day, and I would picture myself running to the mercy seat of God. I would sometimes even act out my entry into His presence, kneeling at His mercy seat. For there, in His presence, I knew I would find my healing. I did this several times a week for three weeks. As I did so, I actually began to feel healing and restoration take place in my life. The time I spent with the Lord in praise and worship and listening to these songs became a time of transition into my complete healing. I could feel it. The process was slow and steady. God was doing a new thing in me, and I knew it!

Vicki Yohé's visit to Covenant Church laid the foundation for me to participate in BOW, "Band of Women," at Covenant Church. Pastor Kathy had introduced this new ministry to our ladies. BOW had come into existence as a result of a conversation Pastor Kathy had with her mother, Molly Parker. Ms. Molly was telling Pastor Kathy that women need to know how to pray. She stressed that women need to be taught how to pray effectively in order for their prayers to reach heaven, the very throne room of God. As Pastor Kathy listened to her mother, God birthed BOW in her spirit. BOW not only gave women the opportunity to strengthen and energize their prayer lives as they infiltrated and overcame the powers of darkness, but BOW also provided women the opportunity to attend classes centered on contemporary, relevant women's issues within the context of a thorough, comprehensive study of God's Word.

The Lord specifically instructed me to attend BOW. He even freed my work schedule so that it was not as booked at that particular time. Consequently, I was able to keep my mornings free so I could attend the prayer time and the class sessions. Pastor Amy Hossler was the teacher of the class, "A Woman's Heart— God's Dwelling Place," the session I had elected to take. (She and her husband, John, are pastors of our children's church and the headmasters of our church school.) Beth Moore authored the class materials. I did not know it then, but God would use this class to supernaturally change my life.

Through Pastor Amy, God taught me to love His Word. As I mentioned earlier, reading my Bible had been one of the biggest challenges in my Christian walk. I would open my Bible and perfunctorily read a Scripture verse or even a chapter, but while I was doing so, I experienced extreme boredom, coupled with an accompanying sense of condemnation and frustration.

All of my Christian life, I had heard how I, as a Christian, needed to stay in God's Word, how powerful the Word was, and so forth. Though I tried, I never seemed to connect with God through His Word. Though reading the Scriptures bored me, still, out of obedience, I faithfully read, hoping for illumination. Admittedly, my disinterested attitude further contributed to my lackluster response to God's Word. Often, I would opt to read Christian literature and books rather than ingest a steady dose of the Bible.

At the first class, Pastor Amy boldly prophesied over all her students that, when we completed her class, we would passionately love God's Word. She firmly believed this and spoke it over us. By the third class, I knew I was in the midst of a dynamic transformation. I found myself reading more chapters from the Bible in just a few weeks than I had thought possible. I studied and studied, yet never wearied. From one to two hours daily, I devoured the Bible. With accompanying workbook in hand, I diligently recorded and studied reference verses as I researched and reveled in *rhema* truths previously foreign to me. (The Greek word *rhema* is often used by Christians to mean a specific word or passage from the Bible that "comes alive" to them when they read it, and through which the Holy Spirit brings them faith, spiritual insight, or direction.) Though each study session would take an hour to two hours to complete, I became oblivious to the passing of time. Facts I once considered dull, I now learned with vigor. My excitement intensified as I drew a picture of the Old Testament tabernacle and memorized the location of the bronze altar, the bronze laver, the golden lampstands, the holy place, and finally the Holy of Holies, where the priest would meet with God, and which contained the ark of the covenant and its mercy seat. I began to understand the ark of the covenant and, most importantly, the mercy seat, which symbolized the presence and atonement of God.

God had already been preparing me for His mercy seat through song and dance. Now, He provided for my eventual freedom from the shackles of my past by enabling me to comprehend, through my study of His Word, the role of the mercy seat in God's forgiveness of His people. As I studied, I would bask in His presence. And, oh, how I loved to be in His presence! As I wept before Him and learned His ways, I was finally able to appreciate His love for me. I did not want to reject anything about Him and wanted everything He had for me. As a result, I was finally able to relinquish my desire to be judge and jury of my life.

Jesus Christ assured me that I was worthy to be forgiven because *He* counted me worthy. I'll never forget the moment that my soul lay bare before Him at my dining room table as I studied one morning in September. My alabaster box was still full, yet some of its contents were being fragmented. An overpowering desire surged throughout my body, and I yearned to give God everything. I knew that, if I released the contents of the alabaster box, I would release the items that I had placed value on, the items that were controlling my life.

Everything that I had considered more valuable than the Lord, I wanted to release and give to Him. Just as the woman in the Bible who had an expensive vial of oil in her alabaster box used it to anoint the Lord Jesus, so I, too, would use the contents of my box as a humble offering to Jesus. I laid all my years of sorrow and shame at the cross of Jesus that morning.

I could feel the love from my Savior flood my soul to the point that I felt a release to finally forgive myself. I actually wanted to forgive Patricia for her failures. I told myself that it was really all right to do this. I could forgive my failures; I didn't have to walk in the condemnation of my past any longer. The pain, anger, failure, impurity, low self-esteem, grief, shame, and unforgiveness all came under the blood of Jesus as I sat at my dining room table and wept and wept. My study guide, my Bible, and my music all ministered to me that day as I accepted my freedom through Christ Jesus. I left my alabaster box at the foot of the cross as I rested before Him. The blood of Jesus had cleansed me and washed me from head to toe. No longer just a verse in the Bible to me, His Word truly was *"a lamp to my feet and a light to my path"* (Psalm 119:105). I could actually see my way clearly. To be in His Word was to be in His presence.

That morning, I had miraculously been healed of my past. Continuously transformed in my inner man, I stayed in Pastor Amy's class for the rest of the three-month course. All these years, I had been missing out on loving God's Word. Now, I finally understood what people meant about the Word! I became saturated in it. I was absorbing His Word, and His Word was absorbing me.

While I was in her class, Pastor Amy played a tape by Integrity Music called *Shout*. The song that most ministered to me was "Jesus, Lover of My Soul." I played that song twenty times a day, if not more. As I did so, its message permeated the very depths of my being, and I knew, without a doubt, that God truly loved my inner man, my soul, the part of me that must constantly die daily. What a blessing to know that God loves the soul of man.

I received deliverance and healing through the power in the blood and the power of God's presence. The strongholds that had prevailed in my life were broken because God's presence took precedence over their very existence. The battle that had been encouraged by Satan for twelve long years, quickly ended in victory as I received the deliverance that had been waiting for me—I had just needed to understand and accept God's complete forgiveness, which was available to me through the blood of Christ. Satan is very territorial, and he hates to give up what he claims to be his personal property—be it the stronghold of shame, guilt, condemnation, or whatever else he is using to control and thwart people. But on that day, deliverance was only a "call of acceptance" away. All I had to do was to receive it. That morning, I did just that, and my life changed forever.

Your change, too, is only a call of acceptance away. All you have to do is make up your mind that you want deliverance from your walls of imprisonment. When I say, "make up your mind," please know that such a decision will usually come to the forefront of your options when you have come to the end of your own journey, your rope, your wits' end, and you are not willing to look back as if you still have unfinished business, or as if you can still make the situation tolerable if you do this or that. "Making up your mind" means that you are ready to exit the prison walls, ready for the chains to fall at your feet, ready to see the key turn in the lock, and finally, ready to exit the cell door that has held you captive. It is at this point that you have really made up your mind to allow God to come in and take over. I cannot explain the peace that comes with accepting deliverance—there is a peace in the soul, a peace in the mind, and a peace in the spirit. I refer to it as Freedom.

The Rhema Word

All of my life I had been taught
By Jesus' blood my life was bought,
Always read my Holy Bible,
Through God's Word would come revival.

So I practiced religiously,
Reading His Word so faithfully.
I thought that God was proud of me,
For taking time to read and study.

But though His Word was in my head,
I didn't absorb the daily bread.
It was not hidden in my heart
To rightly divide His Word apart.

And then one day amid my search
I began to hunger and to thirst
For all that His Word had for me.
I turned each page so desperately.

Soon living waters flowed from me,
And I was shown my destiny.
God's Word in me stood strong and tall;
Down came every fortress and wall.

I forgave myself for what I'd done,
New vision, new life has begun.
Within I know that I am free.
Through the *rhema* word, I have victory!

Chapter Nineteen

The Audible Voice of God

While I was still a student in Pastor Amy's class, the Lord laid it on my heart to do a three-day liquid fast. Inwardly, I felt God calling me to a new area of ministry, but I was unable to identify just what it was. My gifts and talents had formerly been utilized in the area of my creative abilities. I now pondered whether God was calling me to write plays again. I had previously been the drama director with the youth ministry under the pastoral leadership of Pastors Gordon and Derozette Banks, and I wrote skits when I permitted myself to. However, it had become increasingly difficult to maintain my focus in that particular department because I knew God was redirecting me. I wanted to do what He wanted me to do, not what I thought I should do.

On the third day of my fast, a voice awakened me early in the morning. In a gentle yet authoritative voice, I heard the words, "Patricia, it's three o'clock!" I sat straight up in the bed when I heard them and looked at the clock. It was indeed 3:00 A.M. I turned around to my husband to see if he, too, had been awakened, but Eddie was sound asleep. There was no mistake. I had been awakened by the audible voice of God. His voice was recognizable—I knew I hadn't dreamt it. As I fell back on my pillow, I silently whispered, "Lord, is that you?" I waited silently. It was still and quiet once again. What a peaceful feeling, to know that God had awakened me. "But why?" I thought, as I tossed and turned before slowly drifting back to sleep.

When it was time to rise the next morning, I distinctly remembered the still, small voice. So I turned to Eddie and asked him if he had called out my name at 3:00 A.M. I knew that he hadn't, but I just wanted to hear him say no. Eddie confirmed that he had not. I told him what had happened and that I knew it was God's voice speaking to me. However, I didn't have a clue as to what the words, "Patricia, it's three o'clock" meant.

The next morning, when I went to BOW, I wrote Pastor Amy a note explaining what had happened and asking her if she knew what this message meant. I left the note with one of her assistants to give to her. After this, I decided to keep a journal of dates so that I could record anything the Lord might speak to me.

On the night of October 1, as I slept, I was awakened again. But this time it was Satan. He said to me, twice, "Shame, shame." It was the slimiest, most pitiful voice ever. Low in volume, it was spoken directly into my ear, as though he were just inches away. He sounded desperate, as he was fully aware that he had lost his grip on my life. Then he quickly vanished as I called out the name of Jesus. I continued to cast down the words that he had spoken over me. I knew he was trying to put the weight of shame back on my shoulders again. I knew I would have to continue to fight Satan for my right to stay free.

The next morning, I told Eddie what had happened. I told him that Satan was well aware that he had lost and that he was trying to reach out one last time. Speaking "shame" over me no longer had the power it used to. His words were very weak, almost lifeless. Shame had been left at the foot of the cross that morning in September at my dining room table. I refused to pick it up again. However, I could sense the remnants of the tattered veil of shame—it was trying to linger.

If anyone desires to come after Me, let him deny himself, and take up his cross, and follow Me. For whoever desires to save his life will lose it, but whoever loses his life for My sake will find it.
—Matthew 16:24–25

Chapter Twenty

The Powerless Veil of Shame

The Tuesday after I gave Pastor Amy the note, I saw her while I was volunteering at my children's school. She told me that she had received my written message of inquiry and wanted to share with me the symbolism of the three o'clock hour. Pastor Amy stated its prophetic implications. She told me that Jesus had died at three o'clock in the afternoon. Also, she said that those who walk with a prophetic anointing arise at three o'clock in the morning to pray. She said that God often woke her at exactly 3:00 A.M. so she could pray or read. It is an hour God chooses to get one's attention. She stated that it was significant that God spoke this hour of time to me, and she encouraged me to seek His face at three o'clock in the morning.

I wanted to simultaneously run and weep. Oh, that God would speak to *me*—oh, how I loved Him so! God had spoken to me with a specific message! He wanted me to do something. He wanted me, Patricia Harris, a fallen yet restored woman, to do something for Him. I had to share this joy with someone because I knew I could not contain it, it was so overwhelming to me. I then saw Jill, who is also the school director. I went into her office and jubilantly shared my good news with her. I told her how God had spoken to me at three o'clock in the morning. I then recounted to her what Pastor Amy had said. No, I didn't know what God was doing, but God was truly in control. Whatever it was, I was willing to do it. "Here I am, Lord, send me!" was all that my spirit could say in humble surrender.

As the BOW class came to an end, Pastor Amy spoke a prophetic word over the women, a word that I received personally and guarded closely. She prophesied that God was going use us as "firstfruits" in the church, and that God was going to bless us to do "first" things, things that had not yet been done. I held onto that Word. For twelve years, prior to this special time of transition and radical change, I had missed out on what God had wanted me to do. But now I was available, and whatever He wanted to do in me and through me, I wanted as well.

My conversation with Pastor Amy had occurred during the week of Covenant Church's fall revival. I could sense the Enemy trying to remind me in a subtle way of the all-too-familiar shame. I decided I would go up for prayer that night in an attempt to obtain pastoral covering as I continued to release lingering, tattered remnants of the veil of shame. I told Eddie that I was going up to the altar for prayer and my reason, and he joined me in agreement. While at the altar, I asked an usher to beckon Pastor Jessye—the associate pastor who had given Eddie and me counsel regarding the demonic spirits—to come pray with me. He was able to get her attention, and she came over.

Though Pastor Jessye had been aware of my sexual impurity, she had not been informed until now that I had been involved in an affair with a pastor. In short detail, I shared my past with Pastor Jessye. I explained that it had been twelve years since my affair with Pastor, and that I wanted the remnants of the shame to be completely broken off. Pastor Jessye prayed a powerful prayer. She began to violently "break off" in the Spirit the hidden shame of my past and voiced a vigorous prayer of spiritual warfare on my behalf as well. She ministered to me and told me that she always knew God had something great planned for me, but she never said anything because it wasn't time. She expressed that God had given me a spirit of counseling so that I could minister to others.

That night became a milestone in my spirit. It was an enormous leap forward. This time, all the remnants—the entire veil of shame—lay crumpled at the cross. There were no lingering, tattered pieces remaining.

Chapter Twenty-one

Unashamed

The following month, I attended a leadership meeting. The topic being discussed at the close of our meeting centered on transparency with one another and with those whom we lead. Our elders, Wayne and Jill, shared their own personal testimonies regarding their pasts. As they did so, the Holy Spirit suddenly prompted me to openly share about my past in this intimate forum. Before I said anything, I leaned over to Eddie and told him what I felt led to do. He nodded and took my hand.

I interjected that I had a story to share as well. As I began, I became emotional. After twelve years of shame and always feeling that I would die with this deep dark secret hidden inside me, here I sat among leaders in a meeting, about to share the most intimate of details regarding my shameful past. I knew the timing was right, and I knew I was an unashamed woman. God had completely healed me, and I wanted to share what He had done for me. I wanted them to know where I had been and where I was going. The tears streamed down my cheeks, as they so often had in the past when I had referred to this topic, but now I found myself crying for a different reason than before. This time, I cried because I had experienced the healing of God and could now share my deep dark past as a testimony unto Him.

Tears streamed down not only my own cheeks, but also the faces of some of those twelve leaders in the room as they listened intently to my story. I felt such genuine love and acceptance in that room as I told them of my initial refuge center, Christian House of Prayer, then of Covenant Church and Pastors Mike and

Kathy and their effective teaching on a transparent lifestyle. I referred to Pastor Amy's teaching, revealed how Pastor Jessye had broken off the chains of shame, how my oldest sister, Sherrie, stood in the gap, how my parents loved me unconditionally, and most importantly, how Eddie loved me and stood by me through it all.

After sharing my story, a hidden, shameful secret buried inside me for twelve long years, I felt judged by no one, just deeply loved. After I finished, Eddie encouraged me to tell them of my plans to write a book. So I shared with them that I felt impressed in my spirit that God wanted me to share my testimony as a witness to help other hurting women and perhaps, even men, caught in the web of sexual impurity in the church. I was well received that night, and I knew I had embarked on a journey with God. He was indeed taking me somewhere that would require trusting Him and completely giving my all to Him, my heavenly Father. This disclosure in this small setting was just the beginning of the many disclosures to come. Whether or not I would be as well received as I had been at this meeting was questionable. However, to put things in perspective, it was not for me, it was for Him. There would be others who would need to hear my testimony so that their captive souls could also be set free to proclaim an "unashamed" declaration. During subsequent leaders' meetings, my fellow leaders never treated me any differently. It was as if I had never told them. I thank God for His people—for their maturity, unconditional love, and covenant relationship.

That night, after I returned home, I turned to Eddie and told him that I felt like I was on an indescribable high! I explained that it was as if the larger the audience I shared my testimony with, the more grace I felt. I had experienced twelve years—4,380 days of my life—battling with the shame and the unworthiness, but now, as a part of my healing, I walked in the liberty of God's grace to unashamedly and openly share my testimony. Hopefully, one day soon, I confided to my husband, it would be told for the healing of countless others.

In December, as a confirmation of the desires of my heart, the Lord instructed me to write my story during the following January, and that He would anoint me to complete it. In obedience, I blocked out the designated dates in my calendar to begin the writing of my book.

Proclaiming that one is unashamed does not imply that one is in any way proud of his or her shameful past; rather, it is a declaration to the Enemy that states, "I will not be marked as a failure, as one who must wear a veil of shame. I've been bought by the blood of the Lamb and am counted worthy! I will not walk as though I have no hope, for I am victorious. I am unashamed in the eyes of my Father. He is proud of me!"

From Shame...

How can I describe my long journey
from a veil of shame to a veil of glory,
When it has taken twelve years
For me to be able to tell my story?

My mind goes back to just before my fall
To the point where I was caught in between,
Entangled in a whirlwind of flesh and sin,
And a sad life of fantasy and dreams,
Thinking grass was greener on the other side,
Wishing I could taste of the forbidden fruit,
Feeling somehow vibrant and alive,
Willing to accept a lie instead of truth.

When I think back on all my foolish actions,
And the struggle that was yet twelve years ahead,
There is no way that I ever could have known
The shameful path that I was soon to tread.
The truth that is evident in all of this
Is that God turns what is bad to what is good.
Only He can restore the beauty
In something no one else ever could.

to Glory!

For years I wore a veil of shame
Until the time I was released,
Then it was lifted from my heart
And all my torment finally ceased.

On my head God placed a new veil.
Beautiful as the freshly fallen snow.
Trimmed in gold, encircled with pearls
And diamonds sparkling in a row.

Everywhere I now turned my head,
Demons would try to hide their eyes.
They'd yell, plead, and cry for mercy,
The veil's glory their sure demise.

They knew they had lost the battle,
They had to bow before the Name.
Under my feet, all crumpled up,
Was the defeated veil of shame.

"Here! Take it now!" I threw it down,
and it fell limp before their feet.
"Now pick it up and put it on
To wear as your sign of defeat!"

At my command, they put it on,
That wretched veil with which I fell.
"You'll wear the shame from this time on.
Leave me now, and descend to hell."

And so my story ends in victory.
Free at last, no longer ashamed.
I've been washed in redeeming blood.
Purified by His holy name!

Section Four:
Free at Last

Chapter Twenty-two

Hurting People, Healed Lives

D uring the Christmas season, my husband, children, and I went home to share the holidays with my parents and siblings. While we were there, the Lord spoke to me and told me that my ministry to women would connect with the nonprofit organization, Women Who Love God's Way, Inc. (WWLGW), founded by my mother, Mary Cunningham. WWLGW was established to bring spiritual restoration and guidance to hurting women. The theme of this organization, "Hurting Women, Healed Lives," reflects my mother's own tender heart for hurting women.

Always a great mentor who believes the best about everyone, I can still remember the sensitivity in my mother's response when I finally told her about my affair with Pastor. Amid the shock, hurt, and her obvious disappointment, she praised me for getting out of the relationship. Over the years, my mother never rejected me or brought it up as an issue of rebuke. She just continued to love me as she always had. A man of few words, my father simply listened, loved me, and, like Mom, expressed his relief that I had gotten out of the situation. My parents are such jewels. I love them and I am glad they have always been there for me. It is because of their belief in me that they invested in the printing of the first version of this book.

After sharing with my mother concerning the release I felt to write this book, she requested that I be one of the speakers at the WWLGW Annual Conference to be held in the fall of the upcoming year. She wanted me to give my testimony and minister healing in the lives of other hurting women, women who might be dealing with bitterness, shame, self-condemnation, or other painful, often unspeakable, issues from their pasts. Free from my own chains of shame and self-condemnation, I could now look forward with joyful anticipation to the opportunity of sharing and imparting the beauty and reality of God's amazing grace.

God gave me a confirming word a few months before I published the first version of this book. It came through a prophetess named Nancy, who was not aware of my past, and who ministers all over the nation. Nancy, by the Spirit, imparted God's prophetic word to me. I am including here what I feel God has released me to share with you. It is as follows:

> For the Lord says, "Your heart has been healed, and the healing that you have received graciously and freely of Him, you're going to freely give away to others who still have wounds in their hearts. He's going to put their hearts in your hand. And those who would not trust anyone else with this issue of their heart will trust you." The Spirit of the Lord says, "Because they'll see the healing that's in your heart, and they'll desire and hunger and thirst after that for their own lives."

After this word, which was taped, was given to me, I wrote it down word for word as it had been spoken. And God reminded me again of His promise:

> *For I know the thoughts and plans that I have for you, says the Lord, thoughts and plans for welfare and peace and not for evil, to give you hope in your final outcome.*   (Jeremiah 29:11 AMP)

Several months before this prophetic word came to me, I was contacted by the office of Pastors Mitch and Melinda Manning, the pastors for the family development ministry at Covenant Church. I had previously provided Pastor Melinda with a copy of the manuscript for this book so that she could write a prayer as an inclusion. (Her prayer, along with those submitted by others, is included in the Prayers of Agreement section of this book.) Her secretary, Darla, E-mailed me to see if I would share my story in the fall for the Band of Women ministry. I'll never forget the feeling that came over me as I read my E-mail that day. I was never so humbled and so blessed, knowing that I would be able to sow a spiritual seed back into the BOW ministry, the ministry God had foreordained to start the process for my freedom. To minister for BOW was a high honor.

I humbly accepted the invitation. I knew I would title the class, "From a Veil of Shame to a Veil of Glory." I envisioned women being set free by the healing of God's Word. What a privilege that He would take my testimony and use it for His glory. (No wonder the Enemy tried to deceive me with shame. He is such a liar.)

This ministry has become an ongoing one. Now, every time a new session begins, without fail, there are women who register for these classes because they desire to be free. Each woman is seeking to exit her prison walls of shame. It has been a pleasure and a humbling experience to share my story and to minister healing, hope, and restoration to these women and to the women and men I meet at conferences and workshops at which I am asked to speak. In a way, I feel like Harriet Tubman—now that I have escaped to freedom, I am returning to help lead others out of slavery. It is very rewarding, and I am blessed that God has allowed me such a privilege.

Let me share with you a few of the personal testimonies and experiences of those who have attended my classes or other ministry outreaches where I have told my story.

At a ladies' conference, a woman came up to me and was crying almost uncontrollably. She was trying to whisper, but her weeping was making that impossible. She said she was so ashamed about what she had done and that she would be even more ashamed if her mother knew about it. This young lady lived with her mother and loved her very much. She said she wanted desperately to be forgiven but felt unworthy. I hugged her as I prayed a prayer of release over her. I realized that she was struggling with an inability to forgive herself. She would not let her past go. I reminded her that no matter how far she might have fallen, God's arms were not too short to reach her and that He always sees her as His princess.

God says in Isaiah 61:3, 7 that He gives beauty for ashes and that, instead of our former shame, He will give double honor. He is the lifter of our heads (Psalm 3:3). I encouraged this sister with these words, and God lifted her head through His grace. She looked at me and told me that she had already begun reading my book and felt that she, too, had made some of the same wrong choices that I had made. She said she was encouraged by what God had done for me.

Another lady at this conference stood up at the conclusion of the ministry time to share the healing that God had given her. She looked at me and said, "You will never know what you have done for me in this conference." She went on to say that for years she had carried a deep, dark secret, a secret covered in shame. As I listened to her share her testimony, I remembered that this was the same woman who had been crying in the front row throughout most of my ministry time. She continued to reveal her past, and I discovered why she had been crying so intensely. As she told her story, she wept again. It went something like this: "For years, I was in the church. I flirted with the men and particularly the ministers. We would sneak around and sleep together. It was like a game. They all wanted me, and I would go from church to church following the same pattern. 'These ministers have wives, but they do not care about that, so why should I?' I rationalized at the time.

"I continued in this lifestyle until the unthinkable happened—I got pregnant. I could not believe that I had gotten pregnant by one of the ministers in the church. Immediately, I fled the church. No one in the congregation was aware of my lifestyle, and I did not want them to know I was pregnant, so I left in shame. I had my baby, but I continued to live with this shame. I did not want to explain to other people who the baby's father was and how his birth had come about because of the shame I felt. My whole world was changed because of this baby, and I feel I have been running ever since. But today, as you shared your story, God began to deal with my heart. He wants me to stop running and to move forward with what He wants me to do in life. I know God has a purpose for me." This woman pointed toward me and said, "Thank you for being brave enough to tell your story. You have changed my life. I love you and I thank God for you." I was overwhelmed by her transparency and her eagerness for a new beginning. It was for this reason that Jesus was sent into the world — to heal the brokenhearted and to set the captives free.

I am still fascinated by the way God worked out all the details to bring healing to another woman's life. It was early on the second day of a conference at which I was a guest speaker. I was sharing a hotel room with the other guest speaker, an evangelist named Jennifer. We were in our hotel room when a knock came at the door. When I answered it, the woman at the door said that one of Jennifer's assistants needed help. From what I understood, the young lady was downstairs in another hotel room in pain and in tears because of a migraine headache. She wanted Jennifer to come and pray for her.

Jennifer was studying and reviewing her notes for her next message, and she asked me if I would please go and pray for this young lady. I was a little surprised at the request, but I told her I would be glad to. I reached into my purse and took out some aspirin. Then I told Jennifer we would pray, add some practical application, and leave the matter in God's hands.

I went downstairs, and this sister was holding her head in pain and whimpering. I first introduced myself and explained that Jennifer had sent me in her place. I prayed with her, gave her the aspirin, and encouraged her. That evening, before I ministered, I saw the sister. She gave me a hug and thanked me for praying with her. She said she felt much better and that the headache was gone.

At the meeting, I was introduced as the speaker, and I began sharing about myself and giving my testimony. The sister for whom I had prayed was sitting in the front row. I noticed that the more I shared, the grimmer her face became. She tightened her jaw and looked at me with piercing eyes. This made me feel rather uncomfortable. I wasn't sure what was happening with her. I just knew that she did not look very happy, not like the woman I had just hugged less than twenty minutes earlier.

As I continued to minister, I tried not to look at her. Then, without warning, this young lady's countenance began to change and soften. Something had broken within her. She began to weep very intensely, and a few ladies came over to minister to her. I knew God was doing a healing within her.

When the service came to an end, this young lady came up to me and thanked me for sharing my story. Then she became very transparent with me. She said something like this: "When you first started sharing your story, I became very angry with you because my husband had had an affair with another woman. I almost got up and walked out on you. But the Lord told me to stay. I told the Lord, 'I will stay, but I do not have to love this sister.'

"However, when you began to share about meeting the pastor's wife, and when you began to weep as you came to that part of your story, I realized that you were truly sorry for what you had done. That is when I realized that I had been holding onto my anger concerning the affair my husband had with this other woman.

"My husband and I had both been elders in the church, and things had been going so well for us. I loved him very much. After his affair, I decided to pay him back, and I also went out and had an affair. We soon separated, and from that point, I became so depressed that I turned to drugs and became addicted. I was on drugs for many years. Recently, I was in a bad accident, and I still have headaches as a result.

"Evangelist Jennifer met me one day and began to minister to me, and God used her to bring me back to the church. I have just started a ministry helping drug addicts turn to God instead of to drugs. But I hadn't realized I was still struggling inwardly with the heartache of my husband's affair, and that this was causing my physical pain to intensify. The Lord revealed to me that I was still in bondage to my past and that I had to let it go."

This woman then reached out and hugged me and thanked me. I thanked her for sharing her story with me, and I apologized for the pain she had experienced in her past, which had likely been caused by a woman who was weak and wounded, much as I had been. I commended her for her willingness to accept God's grace to forgive.

At the same conference, the theme of which was "transparency," another woman stood up and said that she had been carrying around guilt because of the death of two of her sons. One had been murdered, and the other had been killed in an auto accident. Both had been grown men at the time of their deaths, and this mother appeared to be approaching her mid-fifties. She said she knew that it was not her fault that either son had died but that she had been suffering tremendous guilt over their loss. She said she wanted to be free and that she appreciated the transparency and the anointing that was characterizing the meetings. She said that she, too, had felt a release to let the past go. She thanked me for sharing my story, saying that she was determined not to waste any more time in guilt. God did a special work of restoration in this woman's life.

Recently, I was interviewed about my story for a radio program. The man who interviewed me told me that although men do not often share their feelings about such issues as guilt, shame, and condemnation, they are still troubled by these things. He went on to say that men are "fixers": they would rather try to fix the problem than sit down and talk about the real pain within them. Ministries such as Promise Keepers have been established so that men can talk to other men and say, "These are my issues. Can you help me?" Perhaps more churches should initiate heart-to-heart ministries for men. As men are healed and made whole, the moral fabric of our nation will once again be strengthened in the home, in the church, and in the community at large.

Sheryl Knight is one of my former students from the "Veil of Shame to Veil of Glory" classes. She gave me permission to use her name, and her life is a true success story. When she initially began the six-week class, she was very quiet. I expressed to the students that one of the objectives of the class was that they be able to openly discuss their pasts with one another in confidence. I explained that talking about their past hurts and shame would be a bold step toward walking out of the past and moving forward with their lives.

In the second class, Sheryl asked me, "If I am not able to share my story, will I flunk this class?" I told her, "No, there is no pass or fail in this class." I expressed to her and the rest of the class that the main objective of the course was to provide ministry and to bring healing, to offer a safe and nonjudgmental environment where they could meet others who were challenged with similar issues, and to establish a foundation on which they could walk out of their pasts and into their God-given destiny and callings.

Sheryl was relieved, and said, "Good, because I don't think I can tell my story. I'm just not ready." I assured Sheryl that it was all right and that she was under no pressure.

In our third class, we had an intense ministry time in which there was a powerful move of the Holy Spirit. I cannot explain to you how God comes in and begins to break up the fallow ground; He just does. As I ministered, many of the women in this class wept, and Sheryl was very moved.

We progressed through the fourth class, which focuses on covenant renewal, and we renewed our vows to the Lord as His committed bride. As usual, to illustrate this, we had a "wedding ceremony" in which each woman individually walked down the aisle adorned with a veil and tiara. As she came to stand before the Lord, she took communion, placed a symbolic covenant ring on her on finger, and shared her wedding vows before the Lord as a renewal of her dedication and commitment to Him. After the ceremony, we had a reception with wedding cake and punch. Each girl received pictures of her wedding experience and was encouraged to enjoy her "honeymoon" with the Lord and to let her intimacy with Him endure for a lifetime. This class has proven to be a refreshing experience of renewal for many woman.

In our fifth class, which is a session designed for disclosure and an unveiling of the past, the students are given the opportunity to share their pasts if they so choose. During this class, Sheryl looked at me and said, "I am ready to share," and she shared her story along with the other students. A freeing had taken place in this precious lady's life. God had lifted her head, and she was no longer enslaved by her shame.

Within six months of becoming free and pursuing the heart of God, this woman was in leadership ministry. Do you know what she is doing now? She is one of the leaders of the "Shame to Glory" community outreach ministry, giving other women the opportunity to release the pain and shame of their pasts in an environment of love and acceptance, in the same way she received healing.

God has done a great work in Sheryl's life. She has allowed God's grace and the power of the blood of Christ to accomplish its purpose in her life. She would not be in this position if she had not trusted God and walked out of her imprisonment and into His freedom, where He moved her forward in Him in a ministry of spiritual authority and leadership. It doesn't have to take years and years of our serving God before we can be used by Him. When you let go and are ready to be used by Him, He is ready to put you into the destiny for which you were created from the beginning of time. And remember, your destiny will always be a continually unfolding process. You will never "arrive." God always has more for you to do as you make yourself available to Him.

I would like to share one final story of a precious woman who had seen me on a television interview and called to find out more about the ministry. Her story really touched my heart.

This young lady was a divorced mother of two and was serving God when she met a man whom she cared for very much. She really felt that God had placed this man in her life. However, she fell into a sexual relationship with him and became pregnant. Then she discovered that this man, whom she thought she would marry, was already married and in a leadership position at another church. She was devastated by his lies. However, she turned back to God, asked Him to forgive her for falling and to restore her, and decided to keep the baby. Although her baby was born with an illness, he continues to be a joy to her.

Eventually, the wife of this man found out about the baby, and this young woman had to deal with the resentment of a betrayed wife as well as the father's visitation rights and many other issues. She also lost several jobs because she often had to take time off from work to care for her child. Many times, she had to rush him to the hospital for lifesaving treatment. In addition, she and her children moved over fifteen times in the first few years after the birth of her son.

This woman continued to walk with God and eventually joined my class. I spent time talking with her on the telephone and after class, and I could see that she was still hurting from what had happened to her. She told me that she almost felt forsaken by God. She felt very discouraged because of the difficulty of trying to pay the rent and household expenses while continually losing her job.

She wept with me on several occasions, and I prayed with her and helped her as God led me. But it was during the "wedding" class that this woman experienced a miraculous inner change. She told me that she could not put into words the way she felt and how she knew that God had done a great thing for her and in her. Her comment to me was, "I'm sorry that you fell, but I am glad you got up, because you have picked up so many others. Thank you for what you have done for me by letting God use you." She was bubbling with great joy. I shared with her what I have shared with so many others: intimacy with God is the avenue for your freedom. Stay before Him, worship Him, obey Him, adore Him, serve Him, embrace His ways, live under His anointing, give Him the glory, and you will continue to soar in Him through Christ Jesus.

I believe that God is going to set thousands of people free through this book, just as these woman have been set free. God reigns and Satan loses, once again.

I know in my spirit that those twelve lost years of my life will be redeemed over and over and over again at the expense of Satan's kingdom. He will pay a hundredfold for every day of shame I endured. The exchange will be the equivalent number of souls for the days I lost as a captive to shame. Since I was imprisoned for 4,380 days, Satan will grimace as he sees a minimum of 438,000 captives set free! These women and men will be snatched from the grip of Satan! We will crush his head under our feet, and with a loud shout, we will all declare, "I am healed by the blood of Jesus. I am unashamed!" Each time I get the opportunity to give my victorious testimony to the glory of God, more and more territory will be taken away from Satan. And the gates of hell will not prevail against God's purpose and plan. To God alone be majesty, dominion, and power!

Hurting People, Healed Lives

For hurting people, God has a plan;
You're not forgotten; He understands.
He knows exactly where you've been;
He knows the nature of your sin.

Remember this: He's full of grace,
He wants to know you face-to-face.
You have no reason to run and hide,
It is for your sins His Son has died.

The Devil will try to feed you shame,
So in that state you will remain.
But to him you'll turn a deafened ear,
Push him far; don't let him near.

Let Satan know that you're not worried,
That through God's Son your sins were buried,
That when you pray, your needs are heard.
Remind him of God's faithful Word.

Chapter Twenty-three

Happily Ever After

As my time with you, dear reader, draws to a close, please allow me to reveal some of the hidden secrets that God has since manifested to me. For instance, the Lord told me that the writing of the book you currently hold in your hands was my "three o'clock hour." This is the purpose for which He first awakened me and called my name. In essence, this was my hour to die to self, so that *He* might be glorified. To write this book was to bare my soul, and for Him it has been worth every tear I shed as I traveled back in time to recount my past. Every sin that I laid bare before you has already been laid bare at the cross of Jesus and been covered by His atoning blood. With my veil of shame gone and my veil of glory in place, I can now declare overcoming victory through Jesus Christ. You, too, have a "three o'clock hour." Listen for His voice, and harken to His call. He has not forsaken you.

God explained to me why He chose our daughter's name to be "Amazing Grace." As I mentioned, He told me that she was named as a reminder to me of His truly amazing grace in my life. In the Old Testament, names were given to children for a purpose or as a reminder. For instance, Pharaoh's daughter gave Moses his name because he was drawn out of the water. Hannah named her son Samuel, "Heard of God," because she had asked the Lord for a son and God heard her plea. So it was with our daughter. Her name was given as a reminder to me of His amazing grace in my life and His view of me as His princess.

God's grace also covered me as I wrote this book. Satan tried to discourage me and even tried to attack my children to cause me to lose focus. But through God, our children walked out in victory, and I kept on writing.

At the time of this writing, our oldest daughter, Denyel, has just graduated from high school. She is such a gracious young lady and possesses such fine qualities. Ever since Denyel was a little girl, she has had a heart for God. Though raised with Christian values, Denyel has been challenged in so many ways. We believe the Enemy's plans were to use my divorce from her father as a device to hinder her spiritual growth. As a sensitive and loving child, Denyel always sought to maintain a relationship with her dad. However, over the years, her father did not reciprocate, and Denyel experienced great frustration and rejection over his lack of interest in her and his noninvolvement in her life. Though Satan tried to use this rejection against her, we believe that Denyel became stronger and more committed than ever to walk hand in hand with God. Denyel, too, has a story she can share with other teenage girls, one that will help them stay focused and walk in purity.

We are proud of Denyel. She has encouraged me as I have engaged in the writing of this book. Her main emphasis has been for me to follow the voice of God. She told me once, "I'm not worried about people knowing about your past. I love you, Mom, and you will always be my mother." She further stated, "After knowing more about your story, I have a better understanding of the reasons you have always been so protective of me." Our girl, Denyel, has revealed that God has told her that she will use her gifts of dance and song to glorify Him. She is excited about this new path that God is taking her on and shows more commitment every day to be all she can be for Him. God has great things in store for our daughter.

Our son Earl is now seventeen. He is such a precious jewel to God, and he, too, has been supportive about my sharing my story. Although he initially expressed concern over what others would say about me, he quickly received a revelation regarding how my story would free others from shame. As I shared with Earl the dynamic transformation I had experienced from shame to being unashamed, he became more aware of God's influence in the writing of this book. He was also very touched by the story I shared regarding Eddie's love for me and how he cared for me in spite of my past. I expressed to Earl that Eddie had encouraged me in the writing of my story. Earl, who had never heard the full story of his father's sacrificial love for me until recently, was further convinced that God's purpose and plan regarding the writing of this book must be preeminent. He told me I had his support and his love. Earl is anointed as an oracle for God. He possesses leadership skills and the innate desire to fulfill his purpose and destiny. We expect the manifestation of the call God has on Earl's life to be used as an influence for his peers and other young people.

Amira (Amazing Grace), our youngest, is almost twelve. She understands the importance of purity and knows about my story in general. She is aware that the content of this book is relevant to helping others overcome in the area of shame. Amira is an intercessor and has received a prophetic word that she has the spirit of Esther. In fact, Amira has been interceding for the birth of this book.

As you know, God has given me a wonderful husband, Eddie, a man who has been my covering from the very beginning. He is a man who prays for me and supports me in the ministry God has given me. Eddie and I recently had the opportunity to minister together. After I gave my talk, he got up and shared from his heart about a husband's role as a spiritual covering for his family and as the priest of the home. As God leads, we may do more ministry together to address a range of spiritual issues that affect both women and men. I am blessed as a woman of God in having my husband's full support.

May God enlighten your path and give you sure direction as you step out of your prison walls to walk in the liberty of your freedom through Christ Jesus. He has great plans for you. Don't let Satan bluff you by thinking your sin is too great to reveal. When you shed light on something, it is no longer hidden; rather, it is illuminated and becomes visible for all to see. Where there is light, darkness cannot dwell. Let the light of Christ shine on your hidden secret. Make it known to Him by confessing it, then release it to Him. And Satan, who lives in darkness, will flee because he cannot stand to be in the light.

You are forgiven by God. Now it is time for you to forgive yourself. How? By knowing Him face-to-face through an intimate relationship with Him. Spend time with God, and let His Word permeate your being, your inner man. Thus, you will be able to leave your shame at the cross and walk in victory. And others will overcome by your testimony.

"For this is a prosperous year for us. The doors of success have been opened. We shall succeed in everything in Christ. The door of failure has been closed, and we shall not know defeat. *'And being fully persuaded that, what he ha*[s] *promised, he* [is] *able also to perform'* (Romans 4:21 KJV)."

In the next chapter, I have outlined specific keys to enable you to obtain freedom from your own inner imprisonment and to remain in liberty.

Chapter Twenty-four

KEYS to Your Freedom

Y ou've read my story of how I went from the inner imprisonment of shame to forgiveness and liberty in Christ. I've
tried to take you through each step of my journey in order
to show you how I allowed shame to come into my life, how I
struggled to become free, and how I eventually broke free of my
chains and escaped to a new life. I want to assure you that this
freedom is possible for you, too. In this chapter, I have included
specific keys to overcoming inner imprisonment so that you won't
close this book until you truly know how to enter into freedom
and restoration.

Avoiding Walking into Shame

First, I want to talk about how we can avoid falling into
shame, because we won't have to walk out of shame if we never
walk into it in the first place.

For those of us whose shame was caused by a poor decision we
made, we need to examine why we made this decision. Why did
we make the choice that caused us to become ensnared? Why
didn't we just walk away? We had a choice; no one made the decision for us. We chose a path that seemed greener; however, once we
were securely on the other side, we discovered that it was really a
desert covered with weeds, thorns, and thistles. We also discovered
that it is harder to get out of the desert than it is to get into it.

So, why do we walk into shame? Often, it is because we are
searching. We are looking for something to fill a void that was

made in our lives. A void can come from divorce, abuse, rejection, pain, grief, death, disappointment, and so on. A void becomes a vacuum ready to absorb something. It seeks to be filled, with no regard to what it is filling itself with.

Satan is walking back and forth, *"seeking whom he may devour"* (1 Peter 5:8). When he sees that you are vulnerable, he tries to capitalize on your weakness. If drinking alcohol is your weakness, then Satan will set up a situation in which you can fall into this temptation. He will comfort you with words of deception, provoking you to choose what makes you feel good over what is truly good for you.

We live in a society where divorce is prevalent. If you are experiencing the pain of a strained marriage, separation, or divorce, the Enemy may try to lure you into a circle where there are wounded people who have been divorced but who are wearing masks of happiness, who act as though they were unaffected by their divorces, so that you will be drawn into the same deception. These masks are often worn well and can deceive almost anyone who is vulnerable and seeking companionship. The plan of Satan is to make you judge with your emotions and make decisions by what you see with your eyes alone—what is outward. He likes to make things look good in order to pacify those whose emotions and wills have been weakened through their difficult circumstances. His plan is to divert your attention enough to make you question whether you should return to the promises of God or turn to something tangible, something you can feel and touch. People who are hurting and vulnerable want to be pacified immediately. A yearning takes place within them. If they make the choice to fill this void with something that is not good for them and that God has not provided, guilt will enter the picture. This guilt will then result in shame, which will become a continual reminder of their failure.

Become Aware of Your Weaknesses

Therefore, how can we avoid walking into shame? First of all, we must become aware of our weaknesses so that, when we become tempted to gratify our desires, we can recognize that the Enemy is trying to set us up for a fall.

Fill the Void with the Word of God

Second, people who are hurting due to a sudden disruption in their lives should quickly fill the void with the Word of God. When I say quickly, I mean we must *run* to the Rock that is higher than we are (Psalm 61:2). Instead of seeking to fill ourselves with what makes us feel good, we should seek to find refuge in God's Word and ultimately train ourselves to go to the Word to fill the void and not to get quick "fixes" that entrap our souls.

Make the Decision to Choose the Right Path

It's all about choices, and there are at least two paths. One offers a fulfilling life, the other offers immediate gratification without fulfillment. The choice to do what is wrong is always before us, and it is the easiest path to take. Each time you are faced with a temptation to do wrong, remember that the choice is yours; the results will be the consequences of the choice you make.

The next time you are tempted to sin, make a conscious decision to say no to the temptation. You will more quickly recover from the challenge it took to say no than you will from saying yes to the temptation.

The Word of God can help us through our imprisonment, but we must make the decision to turn to it; otherwise, we will chose a superficial pain reliever that will keep us in captivity.

Avoid Substitutes for True Freedom

However, if we should fall into shame or become paralyzed by our own particular type of imprisonment, we will often find that we go through additional pain trying to find our way out again. As I said before, we discover that it is harder to get out of the desert than it is to get into it. This will often cause us to lose the will to fight our way out, and we will look for alternatives to soothe our pain.

Once we have fallen into shame or are experiencing other types of hurt, we often turn to what I'll call "substitutes." We are all familiar with what substitute teachers are. While they often can be a help in smoothing the transition until the "real" teacher returns, they usually don't operate in the same authority that the teacher does. The teacher who was originally assigned to the class, and has been with the students from the beginning, establishes the course objectives, knows the details of the lesson plans, and implements plans for helping the students overcome the challenges of the material so that they can receive an A as their grade. The substitute teacher is primarily a fill-in until the real teacher returns, and the amount of coursework that is covered and the discipline that is maintained are often less than the normal class routine. Once the real teacher takes his or her place again in the classroom, things are restored to order.

This is similar to the way it is with us when we turn from our true source of spiritual leadership—ending up with disorder and even chaos in the "classroom" of our lives—and we allow substitutes to enter in our attempts to cope with our pain and shame. These substitutes, which are often defense mechanisms, do not operate with the same love, grace, freedom, and self-discipline that come when we abide in Jesus, our real Teacher. Certain substitutes may be of some help to us as we make our way back to restoration in Christ. However, once we allow the real Teacher to return to our life's classroom, He takes His rightful place of authority and brings true order. The classroom is no longer unruly. We can now be transformed and discipled by Him in order to receive our "A," which in spiritual terms is, *"Well done, good and faithful servant; you were faithful over a few things, I will make you ruler over many things. Enter into the joy of your lord"* (Matthew 25:21).

Because we often misunderstand God's way of forgiveness and restoration, some of our substitutes may even appear to be godly ones. In my attempt to become free from my shame, I, too, used substitutes instead of the real authority in my life—God's Word. For instance, as I wrote in chapter 14, I tried "confession." I tried writing a letter to my pastors confessing my past failure, instead of leaving it at the foot of the cross under the blood. The act of confessing our sins to others may be the final link to healing and wholeness for some people, but for me it was a substitute for what I needed to do. Confessing our faults one to another is biblically sound, but not when we are trying to place our burden of shame and guilt on the other person, or if we feel he or she can absolve us of our sin. Confession does not substitute for casting our burdens upon Jesus Christ, and I hadn't fully done that. Christians are to bear one another's burdens, as they are instructed to do according to Scripture, but the ultimate Burden-Bearer is Jesus. Not only does He bear our burdens and our sins, but He also possesses the power to release us from the weight of them all and to bring healing to our lives.

I also tried the "monitoring my walk" substitute. This substitute allowed me to feel as if I were doing God a favor. It was my job to ensure that I did not over-engage in ministry outreach at any level. Since I had been a "fallen woman," I felt there were certain activities and groups from which I should withhold my involvement because of my past. I asked myself, "Would you do this or that if people knew of your past?" That question always called for careful inventory on my part. And without fail, I determined that I was not good enough, spiritual enough, or pure enough to do the "deeper things" of God. Hence, I felt it was my responsibility to police my soul and to govern my ways. This form of self-government became another type of imprisonment for me. I just simply could not escape my past—even in trying to be a good Christian, I boxed myself within a new set of walls—walls that confined me to a checklist of *dos* and *don'ts* in my spiritual walk.

Another of my substitutions for true restoration was the mask of happiness that I wore to appear that I "had it together." The mask was the outer face that covered my inner chaos. It covered up my inner self, who struggled with self-worth, guilt, shame, and condemnation.

Oh, how I fought to maintain a look of spiritual togetherness! True intimacy was such a struggle. I loved my heavenly Father, but I did not want Him to get to close to me because of the secrets in my heart. Nor did I want or allow others to "know" me. Wearing a mask just required that I *act* the part; intimacy would require that I *be* the part. I determined that no one I knew would be allowed to touch the secret place of my heart, for I feared they might reject me, scorn me, criticize me, and look down upon me. It was easier and safer to wear the mask—there was no risk of exposure. Outwardly, I could mingle, fit in, and seemingly be at my best; but inwardly a battle raged, and I felt very isolated from God. I could feel Him drawing me, but I resisted. I dared not become intimate with Him. Therefore, I continued to wear the mask—the loathed mask—as a substitute for freedom.

These three substitutes served as temporary avenues for me to escape a past that was ever before me. But they were never lasting. I used to wonder, "Can I ever be free? Will I ever be free? Or am I doomed to a life where I will seek out substitutes for freedom, micromanage my behavior, and mask my pain?"

The burdens of my past were more than I could bear, and I was driven to find refuge from the storm. As I pursued God's presence, He became my hiding place. No longer did I have to hide within myself; I found I could hide in Him. He became the covering that shielded me from my past. Suddenly, there was a gulf between me and the former me, and I knew that a change had occurred. I was a free woman, with a past that was no longer controlling me.

Recognize and Let Go of Destructive Patterns

Ironically, as much as we want to be rid of destructive patterns in our lives, we tend to cling to them because we're used to them. When I think back to my time of imprisonment, I realize how much I allowed the triplets guilt, shame, and condemnation to govern my life. As much as I wanted to be free of them, I struggled just as much with the thought of who I would be without them. My identity had become entwined with them. I had become accustomed to making decisions based upon these three influences in my life, and I had no concept of how I would manage without them. I wondered what would replace them if they were absent from my life.

I realize now that I had developed a pattern of coping—a pattern that had grooved certain behaviors and reactions into my personality. I was deceived by what appeared to be my true self, but really wasn't. The thought of letting go of what was familiar to me seemed foreign and risky. I was more comfortable holding onto what I knew, even if what I knew was working against me.

I have ministered to many people who want to let go of the patterns to which they are enslaved. It is not that they don't realize that these patterns are working against them; it is just that they feel comfortable and safe with them. Change seems risky. However, to become free of imprisonment, we need to recognize and let go of these destructive patterns and trust Jesus to make us new creations in Him. He is all knowing and all powerful, and He alone can take our fears, our ingrained reactions, and our patterns and replace them with His ways. *"For God has not given us a spirit of fear, but of power and of love and of a sound mind"* (2 Timothy 1:7).

Trusting Him instead of ourselves is the risk. But I assure you, it is a risk worth taking. Please allow Him to be the pattern by which you are governed. It is through Him, in Him, and by Him that we can be set free from whatever has been keeping us entrapped.

K-E-Y-S

I now want to share with you some specific principles for obtaining your freedom. I call them the KEYS that open the door of captivity and lead to freedom. These are not substitutes. They are the real thing, and have proven to set people free.

K **Know** God—become intimate with Him. Remember how, as I moved toward complete freedom from my past, I worshipped Him through dance and song? I would play worship music over and over again. I would also dance in His presence. Little did I realize that I was preparing my heart to know Him. How I wanted Him to touch me in the secret places. I wanted the darkness, the silence, and the whispers of my past to exist no longer. I wept before Him often as I prayed and told Him I wanted to be free. Sometimes, I would sit before Him and never utter a word. I would just cry and lift my hands as high as I could, as though I were trying to touch Him in the heavenlies. It was during these times of worship, prayer, and weeping that I knew I was discovering a God whom I had never known before, the God who sent His Son to make it possible for me to be free. I was willing to spend the time to know Him, to bare my soul in order to be with Him, and to risk my fears so that

167

I could be open and exposed in His presence. I became passionate for Him. I was willing to let Him into the darkest places of my life. Finally, I became not only willing but also deeply desirous to know Him in the beauty of His holiness.

I love You fervently and devotedly, O Lord, my Strength. The Lord is my Rock,...my keen and firm Strength in whom I will trust and take refuge, my Shield, and the Horn of my salvation, my High Tower....In my distress [when seemingly closed in] I called upon the Lord and cried to my God; He heard my voice out of His temple (heavenly dwelling place), and my cry came before Him, into His [very] ears....The Lord rewarded me according to my righteousness (my conscious integrity and sincerity with Him); according to the cleanness of my hands has He recompensed me....As for God, His way is perfect! The word of the Lord is tested and tried; He is a shield to all those who take refuge and put their trust in Him. For who is God except the Lord? Or who is the Rock save our God?...The Lord lives! Blessed be my Rock; and let the God of my salvation be exalted....Therefore will I give thanks and extol You, O Lord, among the nations, and sing praises to Your name. (Psalm 18:1–2, 6, 20, 30–31, 46, 49 AMP)

Escape through His Word, as I mentioned earlier. When I started on my journey to restoration, I began to read and read and read His Word. I devoured it into my spirit. My inner man began to grow in spiritual strength and stature. Something took place in me that I can only explain in one way—it was as if my spirit ignited. The Word of God suddenly became powerful in my life to the pulling down of demonic strongholds (2 Corinthians 10:4) that had once been a vice around my neck. When I would lie down at night, His Word would be upon my lips. When I would awaken, I would awaken to His peace. For twelve years, I had been without peace, and suddenly, peace was upon me, in me, and all around me. As Bible teacher Joyce Meyer often says, "There is life in the Word." The life in the Word became alive in me, and once it became *rhema* (the living word), I was never the same. I knew that I belonged to God and that I would allow nothing to separate me from His love again.

KEYS to Your Freedom

Therefore, [there is] now no condemnation (no adjudging guilty of wrong) for those who are in Christ Jesus, who live [and] walk not after the dictates of the flesh, but after the dictates of the Spirit. For the law of the Spirit of life [which is] in Christ Jesus [the law of our new being] has freed me from the law of sin and of death....For [the Spirit which] you have now received [is] not a spirit of slavery to put you once more in bondage to fear, but you have received the Spirit of adoption [the Spirit producing sonship] in [the bliss of] which we cry, Abba (Father)! Father!...For I am persuaded beyond doubt (am sure) that neither death nor life, nor angels nor principalities, nor things impending and threatening nor things to come, nor powers, nor height nor depth, nor anything else in all creation will be able to separate us from the love of God which is in Christ Jesus our Lord.

(Romans 8:1–2, 15, 38–39 AMP)

You must accept what God says about you. After God's Word became *rhema* to me, I immediately accepted what God had to say about who I was in Him. It was as simple as just believing it. I did not question it. Everything that He said I was, I was. All that He said I could be, I would be. All that He said was forgotten, never existed. The old had passed away, and I was now new—a brand new woman with a new identity through Christ. Being restored was a greater experience in my life than when I first became born again. For now I knew, without a doubt, even after all my failures, that He still held fast to His Word, "I know the plans that I have for you, plans to give you hope and a future, not to bring evil upon you." (See Jeremiah 29:11). The plans that He had for me when I first met Him were the same plans He had for me after my "fall." His plans for my success never changed. In fact, I believe they became bigger and gained a greater purpose, because the Enemy has to pay when he touches one of God's anointed. Whatever my Father says about me in His Word, it is so. I believe it, and I receive it. Amen.

Since all have sinned and are falling short of the honor and glory which God bestows and receives. [All] are justified and made upright and in right standing with God, freely and gratuitously by His grace (His unmerited favor and mercy), through the redemption which is [provided] in Christ Jesus, whom God put forward [before the eyes of us all] as a mercy seat and propitiation by His blood [the cleansing and life-giving sacrifice of atonement and reconciliation, to be received] through faith. This was to show God's righteousness, because in His divine forbearance He had passed over and ignored former sins without punishment.

(Romans 3:23–25 AMP)

Now to Him who, by (in consequence of) the [action of His] power that is at work within us, is able to [carry out His purpose and] do superabundantly, far over and above all that we [dare] ask or think [infinitely beyond our highest prayers, desires, thoughts, hopes, or dreams] — to Him be glory in the church and in Christ Jesus throughout all generations forever and ever. Amen (so be it).

(Ephesians 3:20–21 AMP)

S**elf-forgiveness** is essential, and you must learn to walk in it. This is a difficult challenge of imprisonment that can be overcome only by the Word. I continually battled with forgiving myself. I would not accept the fact that my particular sin could be covered by the blood. But *you must believe it.* The blood of Jesus is our redemptive source. Part of what it means to come to a place of letting go and forgiving yourself and others is through loving God, His Word, and yourself. The ability to acquire such love comes through applying the K-E-Y factors above: knowing God, escaping through His Word, and accepting what God says about you. When you have applied these principles, then you are ready for self-forgiveness. I have found the path of forgiveness to be a step-by-step process of walking through it until you are ready to let your pain and shame go. And, when you are ready, God's grace is sufficient to help you reach the end of the path.

I remember so vividly the morning that I sat at my dining room table wondering if I could release myself from my past failure. I struggled with whether it was fair to be released; I struggled with feeling guilty for wanting to be free; and I was challenged with taking God at His Word. But ultimately, I chose to believe God. I made the decision to trust Him because of the new relationship that I had found in God and because His Word had filled me with so much of Him and His love that I could finally love myself to the point of forgiveness. It was a process for me, and it may be for you, but God has put certain things in place to help us through the process. He is committed to our success.

> *And those whom He thus foreordained, He also called; and those whom He called, He also justified (acquitted, made righteous, putting them into right standing with Himself). And those whom He justified, He also glorified [raising them to a heavenly dignity and condition or state of being]. What then shall we say to [all] this? If God is for us, who [can be] against us? [Who can be our foe, if God is on our side?]* (Romans 8:30–31 AMP)

Jesus has provided these KEYS to staying free. Keep them with you at all times so that you can gain your freedom, and so that you will not be locked up again in captivity. My journey took twelve years of a wilderness experience. There is no way that I would ever want to travel that road again, and I expressed such feelings to the Lord. He quickly impressed upon my spirit that the keys that it took for me to *become* free are the keys that it will take for me to *stay* free.

The Enemy is very cunning, and he will try to make you and me both feel that, since we are free, we can now slack off and get comfortable in our freedom experience. To that I say, "No way." With freedom comes the responsibility to know God even more. Your freedom is not a right that you have earned in the Spirit. Your freedom is not only for the sake of your peace of mind, but is also provided so that you may fulfill your purpose in Him.

Our freedom gives us the liberty to soar like an eagle to higher heights and deeper depths through Christ Jesus. We must pant for Him as the deer pants for the waters (Psalm 42:1), and we must never stop panting for His presence. Your escape must always be to and through His Word, so that you will become replenished, revived, and renewed in Your mind. Then you will keep your mind clear to remember what He says about you, so that you can believe that you can achieve the very thing He has called you to do.

It is that purpose, that call, that destiny, that yet waits for you to pick up your cross and follow Him. I will always treasure what Pastor Jessye Ruffin said to me as I sat in her office discussing the writing of this book. "Many have not yet eaten because you have not taken your place at the table. They are yet waiting to be served what only you can give them." She was referring to the ministry and the call that God has on my life. My freedom makes it possible for me to take my place at your table today, dear reader, to serve you the message of restoration through Christ Jesus. And your freedom will allow you to take your place at the table and serve others who are waiting for what you have to offer. Remember, self-forgiveness, as well as forgiving others, is essential for your success.

> *And I am convinced and sure of this very thing, that He who began a good work in you will continue until the day of Jesus Christ [right up to the time of His return], developing [that good work] and perfecting and bringing it to full completion in you....Now I want you to know and continue to rest assured, brethren, that what [has happened] to me [this imprisonment] has actually only served to advance and give a renewed impetus to the [spreading of the] good news (the Gospel).* (Philippians 1:6, 12 AMP)

Taking a Sure Step of Faith

In closing, I want to encourage you to take a step of faith for your healing and for the pursuit of your God-given destiny. God will use your life, even your past hurts and failures, to fulfill your calling as you respond to His leading in trust and faith.

Let me give you an illustration from my life, because I really want you to get the truest picture of the process by which my walk with Christ has unfolded into transparency, and the faith that it took for me to draw my story from my heart and put it into writing.

Not knowing what the response would be, I literally took up my cross, followed Him, and wrote this book. I trusted the leading of the Holy Spirit, because I believed that He was unfolding a plan that I would only fully understand at the time of its unfolding (along with everyone else). In other words, when I first began to write this book, I had no promises that I would receive a favorable response, that I would begin to have book signings at various churches, or even radio, television, and newspaper interviews. I had only hoped and prayed that I would be given the opportunity to be published by a well-known publisher. I received over fifteen to twenty rejections from publishers when I initially began to send out the manuscript (I still have all my rejection letters). After so many rejections, I then decided to self-publish, because I had no choice if I wanted to share my story and accomplish the mission that God had placed on my heart to minister to hurting people still held captive to their past.

I did not know that God would give me favor with bookstores and that several would place my book on their shelves on a consignment basis, that Paul Jones of T. D. Jakes ministries would believe in my book, place it in the Potter's House bookstore, and then later refer me to Whitaker House, the publisher of this new edition of the book.

It is vitally important to me that you understand that, although this new version of the book includes various testimonies of lives that have been changed and impacted as they have heard my story and the principles for being restored, it was not so until I stepped out in faith—without knowing the outcome ahead of time—and wrote my story. I would not have had any testimonies for this new version if it had not been for my releasing the first version in faith.

My point is that, when things appear risky, and it takes faith to even step out, it is important to do so when you feel the prompting of the Holy Spirit. The call of God on our lives is more important than, "What will people say? What will they think? How will this make me look?"

To me, the first version of this book was my seed of faith; it was the beginning of the ministry that God will give me through this second edition, which will reach a greater audience than the initial book ever could have, because my resources were so limited. Yet, because it was the heart of God, and my calling, God used it and lined up everything to unfold according to His time, will, and purpose.

I really want to encourage you that God can use your past as a foundation for your future ministry—that hiding your past could be hindering your future. Stepping out in faith doesn't come with certain guaranteed promises; it just comes with knowing that God has said to do it. Though you may be reluctant, as I was, God honors obedience, and He will give us the inheritance to which we are due. God is faithful to do what He has promised. Eyes have not seen, nor ears heard, what God has in store for those who love Him (1 Corinthians 2:9).

As I minister to people, they all seem to carry the same hidden message, "Can God use me with my past?" They are fearful to step out for fear of rejection. But, in all honesty, I was fearful of rejection, too. Not knowing the outcome, I believed and trusted God, because He knew the outcome. That isn't something I can take any credit for. With great anxiety, I believed and obeyed. And there may be others who, with great anxiety, have to take the leap of faith to see the unfolding of the significant plan God has for their lives. Faith and obedience are relevant to God; even if we do obey with great anxiety, He puts the emphasis on the fact that we are believing and obeying.

God remains faithful as He seeks the lost, the brokenhearted, the wounded, and those held in captivity. He seeks to restore. He promises to give us double honor for our former shame. I urge you to follow these keys to your freedom, stepping out in faith and obedience. You will never be the same!

The following section includes prayers to enable you to talk to God about your inner imprisonment and to bring you into restoration and peace through Jesus Christ. I urge you to pray the prayer or prayers that best fit your own situation and to take this step to freedom. I speak the blessings of the Lord upon you as you experience deliverance and freedom through Christ Jesus.

Prayers of Agreement
for Healing and Restoration

God directed me to request godly spiritual leaders that I respect to write prayers of agreement that you can pray over yourself as you seek to walk out and stay out of sexual impurity or other types of imprisonment. If you have ever experienced the shame of sexual impurity or the shame of failure, then agree with the prayer that is most applicable to your current situation. Know that God has a specific purpose for your life. Don't succumb to the voice of Satan when he tries to remind you of your past. You are commissioned by God to fight him, destroy him, and take back what he has taken from you, and then to expect a hundredfold return!

The following prayers are for individuals who read this book and see themselves in its pages. Many of these prayers were written by pastors' wives, one was written by my very own mother, and one I wrote myself. Please apply them to your own life, and be healed! The Enemy will try to rob you of your peace, your victory, and your healing; and if you let him, he will try to sway you from or even ruin your destiny. Don't allow him the opportunity! Be set free and walk in your own veil of glory as the bride of Christ.

A Prayer Reflecting God's Faithfulness
(Prayer of Repentance)
by Evangelist Mary Cunningham

FATHER GOD, I come before Your throne room of grace, and in Your presence I lie at Your feet. Only You can wash me from all my ungodly deeds and from all impure thoughts. Father, I realize that You love me and You said that though my *"sins be as scarlet, they shall be as white as snow; though they be red like crimson, they shall be as wool."*[1]

Lord, I thank You for Your cleansing blood. I am submitted to You, and I invite You to come in and give me a clean heart and renew a right spirit within me.

Father God, thank You for letting me know that if I call on Your name and believe in my heart, I shall be saved.[2] Thank You for telling me through Your Word that if I come to You, You will in no wise cast me out.[3]

As I read Your Word and walk in obedience, I know You will direct me and empower me to live a victorious life through You. I will no longer succumb to the desires of my flesh. My desires will be Your desires. I will turn to You for strength when I feel weak. Please give me the wisdom to defeat Satan when he tries to attack me. I will hide Your Word in my heart[4] and will allow it to be *"a lamp to my feet and a light to my path."*[5] I am no longer defeated; I walk as one who knows my place in Jesus. I am the righteousness of Christ.[6] In You and through You, I am victorious.

Thank You for delivering me out of a world of darkness. I will worship You all the days of my life. You alone are worthy, Father, and it is for You that I live. I love You, Lord.

Amen.

---

[1] Isaiah 1:18 KJV; [2] Romans 10:9; [3] John 6:37 KJV; [4] Psalm 119:119; [5] Psalm 119:105; [6] 2 Corinthians 5:21

A Prayer for the Imprisoned Heart
(Freedom from Various Types of Imprisonment)
by Patricia Harris

FATHER, because You are a faithful, loving God, I know that I can boldly come before Your throne of grace and make my requests known before You.[1] Your Word says that I shall call upon You, and You will answer me; that You will be with me in trouble and that You will deliver me and honor me.[2] Father, I come to You in the name of Your Son Jesus. My heart has a secret place, a place of captivity, where I see the darkness and feel the emptiness. It is a place I have not allowed You to touch. But today, Father, I invite You to go into the deepest recesses of my heart where You will find my secrets, where You will see the painful memories, and where You will see the darkness. It is in this place, Father, that I call upon You to bring light, to bring healing, and to bring peace.

You are my Refuge and my Fortress; it is on You that I lean and trust.[3] I will lift up my eyes to the hills where I can see You face-to-face.[4] I want You to look into my heart and "know" me. Under Your shadow there is stability. Dwelling in Your presence puts me into the secret place where You abide.[5] I long to be in a secret place with You, where there is no fear of evil and there are no shifting shadows.[6] There is a hiding place in You that I must run to; it is there that I will find safety.

Prepare my heart, Father, to look toward heaven, so that I may forget those things that are behind and press toward the things that are before me.[7] Your promises are sure and amen,[8] and You have promised me through Your Word that You have plans to give me hope and a future, not evil.[9] So Father, this day, let it be so. May the plans that You have for me unfold as I yield myself as a vessel of honor to be used for Your kingdom. Forgive me for believing that my past was more powerful than the power in the

---

[1] Hebrews 4:16; [2] Psalm 91:15; [3] Psalm 91:2; [4] Psalm 121:1–2; [5] Psalm 91:1; [6] James 1:17 NIV; [7] Philippians 3:13–14; [8] 2 Corinthians 1:20; [9] Jeremiah 29:11

177

shed blood of Jesus. May the blood redeem my soul, and the mercy seat, my past. Give me the grace to forgive myself and others, so that there is an open channel between You and me. I speak freedom to my inner man; I speak the light of God over every dark area of my life, and I command my soul, body, and spirit to come in agreement with the purpose of God for my destiny. I am submitted to You this very day and this very hour. In Jesus' name, Amen.

Prayer of Repentance for the Single
(Spirit of a Virgin)
by Pastor Melinda Manning

FATHER, I come to You now, in the name of Jesus, repenting for the sin of unforgiveness in my life. Your Word tells me that if I confess my sin, You are faithful and just to forgive me and cleanse me of all unrighteousness.[1] Jesus, I confess my unforgiveness toward myself and those who have hurt me. From this moment on, I choose, as an act of my will, to forgive myself for hurting others and violating my own body, which is the temple of Your Holy Spirit. I also choose to forgive the other person(s) who participated with me in this sin.

Satan, I bind every evil spirit that would come to bring condemnation and try to keep me tied to my past. I loose the peace of God to flood my soul and erase those scars. May they serve only as a reminder of God's faithfulness to forgive.

I break every soul-tie with those with whom I have sinned, and I take back those parts of me that I gave away. I take these scattered pieces and present them to You for You to restore to wholeness. I will hold onto my restored purity, and I will not have sexual relations until I am able to give myself to the mate that You have chosen for me.

Thank You, Father, for the cleansing blood of Jesus that washes me white as snow.[2] I ask You now to give me the spirit of a virgin, and I will live in purity all the days of my life.

In Jesus' mighty name, Amen.

---

[1] 1 John 1:9; [2] Isaiah 1:18

A Prayer for Self-Forgiveness
(The Unashamed Woman or Man)
by Pastor Amy Hossler

FATHER GOD, I thank You that You are the God of restoration, a God who loves me so much that You gave Your only Son so that I might be restored through forgiveness. Father, I know that a lack of forgiveness blocks the flow of kingdom power. I know that Your Word says that I should forgive those who offend me, since You forgave me.[1] So I ask You, Holy Spirit, to enable me to choose to forgive.

Father God, Your Word says that as far as the east is from the west, so far have You removed my transgressions from me.[2] Right now, I take You at Your Word, and I ask You to forgive me for all the wrong choices and all the selfish desires that led me to choose to satisfy my flesh and need for approval. I ask that, right now, You would help me to forgive myself. Lord, help me to forgive myself for defiling Your temple, my body. Help me to forgive myself for enjoying the pleasures of the flesh. Help me to forgive myself for the deceptive pride of being desirable. I know, Father God, that You cleanse me for service to You and that You do not desire to leave me with the guilt of this past sin.[3] Your Word says, *"If our heart does not condemn us, we have confidence toward God."*[4] Therefore, I forgive myself for my sin because You paid the price for me. Thank You, Father, for forgiving me through the blood of Jesus.

I also now choose to forgive _____. Lord, I realize that even though my resentment may be justified, it will only hurt me if I choose not to forgive him/her. I forgive _____ for taking advantage of my vulnerability and my weak will. I forgive _____ for not being strong enough to make right choices, even when I didn't make right choices. I refuse to hold a grudge toward _____, and Jesus, I release him/her into Your hands right now. I ask, Lord, that You would lay the ax to the root of any bitterness or resentment that may be in my heart.[5]

---

[1] Matthew 6:12, 14–15; [2] Psalm 103:12; [3] Hebrews 9:14; [4] 1 John 3:21; [5] Matthew 3:10

Because of Your great mercy, Lord, I receive by grace Your forgiveness. And by Your great mercy and grace, I choose to forgive those who have hurt me. I declare Your Word that, instead of shame, I will have double honor.[6] Therefore, by Your grace, I declare that I am an unashamed woman/man. I cry out as the psalmist David did,

Create in me a clean heart, O God,
And renew a steadfast spirit within me,
Do not cast me away from Your presence,
And do not take Your Holy Spirit from me.
Restore to me the joy of Your salvation,
And uphold me by Your generous Spirit.
Then I will teach transgressors Your ways,
And sinners shall be converted to You.[7]

Thank you, Father God, that I am forgiven and that You will use even my failures to ultimately lead others to Your merciful love. In Jesus' mighty name, Amen.

---

[6] Isaiah 61:7; [7] Psalm 51:10–13

A Prayer of Displacement
(Fearfully and Wonderfully Made)
by Pastor Derozette Banks

FATHER, I confess that I have believed the lies and deceptions of Satan when he told me I had to engage in illicit sexual relationships in order to feel loved or to have value. Father, I repent.

Father, I repent for rejecting Your perfect love and settling for the unsatisfying lust of Satan that he gave as a counterfeit, which brought me pain and rejection.

I confess that I am fearfully and wonderfully made,[1] and I am not rejected, but have been *"accepted in the Beloved,"* who is Jesus Christ.[2] I choose to walk in the truth of Your love, Father.

Father, I believe that every good and perfect gift comes from You[3] and that You do not want to withhold anything good from me.[4] The love I long for and have searched for illegitimately I now look to You to fulfill.

Father, You are greater than any void I feel in my heart. I ask You to come and fill that void now. I ask You, Holy Spirit, to come and displace any dysfunctional personality trait, such as being overly sophisticated, extremely shy, promiscuous, shameful, insecure, haughty, jealous, envious, controlling, rejected, angry, lustful, addicted, rebellious, and worthless.

I choose to no longer cloak myself in these traits.

Holy Spirit, come and wash over me, cleanse me, purify me, and clothe me in Your robe of righteousness. Renew my mind with peace and purity. Heal my emotions with Your security and strength. I choose to walk in Your healing and wholeness, no longer in brokenness. Father, You alone satisfy me, and I will follow after You. Amen.

---

[1] Psalm 139:14; [2] Ephesians 1:6; [3] James 1:17; [4] Psalm 84:11

A Prayer for Destroying Soul-Ties
(Restoration and Covenant with God)
by Pastor Jessye Ruffin

LORD JESUS, I confess that I have morally sinned against You and participated in sexual uncleanness. I now understand that I am a *"living sacrifice"*[1] created in Your image and for Your glory. I recognize that I have been purchased by the blood of Jesus and my life is no longer my own.[2] I ask you to forgive me for my sin and to cleanse me from all unrighteousness.[3] Lord, I forgive _____ for his/her participation in this sin. I now sever the soul-tie formed between me and _____, and I also call back into my being all parts of my soul that are now resident within _____. Lord, I send back to _____ everything we shared illicitly in our souls. I forgive all hurt and rejection, and I also release all disappointments suffered in the relationship. Father, I release _____ and speak Your blessing upon him/her. I receive Your forgiveness and restoration and make a covenant with You this day to live my life to Your glory. This day, I receive the spirit of virginity into my own soul and spirit and make a commitment to forever cultivate purity in my life and in the lives of my descendants. Amen.

---

[1] Romans 12:1; [2] 1 Corinthians 6:19–20; [3] 1 John 1:9

Afterword to the Reader

Dear Reader,

God has been with me day by day over the past twelve years. He was with me in every valley and during every storm. The Holy Spirit was ever present to guide me, and the blood of Jesus was always available to free me. Where would I be if He didn't love me? Where will you be if you continue on your present course? I urge you to start now and take your first steps to freedom by trusting in God's love and following the liberating keys in this book.

I want to make sure you understand that God's restoration of my life was not an exception to the rule. God is in the restoring and healing business. He has an abundance of grace and love for anyone who comes to Him. God shows no partiality, and He'll do for you what He has done for me. "There is no question so fearful that God can't answer it, and there's no pit so deep that God isn't deeper." These are the words of a concentration camp survivor, author Corrie ten Boom. In a spiritual and emotional sense, we can be truly imprisoned. But as Corrie found out, it is in the darkest times of imprisonment and fear that we come to know the depths of God's love and His unlimited power and grace to free us from our inner chains.

As you break free from the chains of your past, please feel free to share my testimony with others and to recommend *Imprisoned by Secrets of the Heart* as a vital resource for those seeking to be free from their hurts and shame. Take these words to heart:

The people the Lord has freed will return and enter Jerusalem with joy. Their happiness will last forever. They will have joy and gladness, and all sadness and sorrow will be gone far away.
(Isaiah 51:11 NCV)

185

Since we have been made right with God by our faith, we have peace with God. This happened through our Lord Jesus Christ, who has brought us into that blessing of God's grace that we now enjoy. And we are happy because of the hope we have of sharing God's glory. (Romans 5:1–2 NCV)

Instead of your [former] shame you shall have a twofold recompense; instead of dishonor and reproach [your people] shall rejoice in their portion. Therefore in their land they shall possess double [what they had forfeited]; everlasting joy shall be theirs. (Isaiah 61:7 AMP)

Thank you for taking the time to read my story and its victorious ending. Yet in so many ways, it is an unfinished book. The greatest chapters are yet to be written. They are about your own life. You, too, will walk in victory. It is inevitable. God has inspired this book so that you will walk out of your shame, and move *"from glory to glory"* (2 Corinthians 3:18). God bless you, my friend.

"Only God can take our failures
and make them shine in the
face of the Enemy."

May the purpose and intent of this book accomplish what it was sent forth to do, according to the plan and will of God, our Father. Amen.

—Patricia C. Harris

Acknowledgments

I would like to thank the following women who submitted a prayer for inclusion in this book: Evangelist Mary Cunningham, Pastor Melinda Manning, Pastor Amy Hossler, Pastor Derozette Banks, and Pastor Jessye Ruffin. Please know that your prayers will impact countless lives for eternity.

To my siblings, who kept loving me, kept believing in me, and who never shunned me because of my failures, I say thank you, Sherrie, Rhonda, and Billy. And thank you for the skills and encouragement you contributed to this project. A special thank-you to Sherrie, who edited the first version of *Imprisoned.* Your editorial skill and style enhanced its quality. Thank you for juggling your schedule and meeting the deadlines. You have always stood beside me and supported me. Thank you for being there once again. And to your husband, Jim, thank you for sharing Sherrie during the times I needed her most. To Billy, my dear brother, as a screenwriter, your knowledge and insight have been invaluable. Thank you for your advice and for taking the time to review my work. Rhonda, little sister, thank you for always believing in me. To her husband, Ira, thank you for your comments and review. I love you all.

How can I ever thank you, Paul Jones? You became a beacon of light that paved the way for my entrance. You felt the heartbeat of my message, and you instinctively knew that it was the heartbeat of God. Thank you for opening the door. I am eternally grateful.

Special thanks to Robert Whitaker, Sr., Jim Rill, and Sharon Hemingway of Whitaker House Publishing. You took the time to hear the cry of my message, "Set the captives free!" and then you proceeded to make it known to the world. Thank you for publishing my story so that others can escape from being "imprisoned." God bless you.

From one writer to another, I want to thank Lois Smith, my editor. You have been God appointed and anointed in the editing of this book.

To Pastors Mike and Kathy Hayes, thank you for the corporate mantle of grace, love, and transparency through which you operate, and which manifests and flows throughout our church body. Your ministry on the power of transparency has been *rhema* for me and, consequently, life changing.

To Bishop Nathaniel and Pastor Valerie Holcomb: Christian House of Prayer became a refuge center for me, a shelter from the storm. Your ministry and your unconditional love initiated the foundation for my return to the kingdom of God.

Thank you, Pastor Jessye Ruffin; you have been there to walk with me through the emotional turbulence I experienced as a result of soul-ties and the presence of darkness in my life. Thank you for your counseling and your guidance. Pastor Jerry Ruffin, I want to thank you for your spiritual insight and your warfare. You both have been my mentors and my friends.

As my elders, Wayne and Jill Blue, you have covered me in prayer and stood by me as I shared the progressive stages of this book.

Zone 1 Leaders, thank you for setting the atmosphere that released me to share my story in your presence.

Pastor Amy, my teacher, mentor, and friend: Thank you for adhering to the voice of God as you obediently ministered to the Band of Women. Your impartation of God's Word has changed my life for eternity.

Leeann Morris, thank you for loving me without reservation and for seeing my heart from an angle of love. You are a special friend.

Marcus and Joni Lamb, you heard my testimony, and you opened the door for me to share it on Daystar Television Network; hence, many more doors have opened as a result. I thank you both.

Don and Autumn Spear, it was a divine appointment that allowed our paths to cross. Thank you for your referral; it was the passageway God used to place me in the speaking circuit to strategically pull down the strongholds of shame that the Enemy uses in so many people's lives.